FIXIN' TO BE TEXAN

HELEN BRYANT

Illustrations by Chris Smith

Republic of Texas Press

Published by Republic of Texas Press
An imprint of The Rowman & Littlefield Publishing Group, Inc.
4501 Forbes Boulevard, Suite 200
Lanham, MD 20706

Distributed by NATIONAL BOOK NETWORK

Library of Congress Cataloging-in-Publication Data

Bryant, Helen.
  Fixin' to be Texan / Helen Bryant
    p. cm.
  ISBN 1-55622-648-9 (pbk.)
    1. Texas—Description and travel—Miscellanea. 2. Texas—Social life and customs—Miscellanea. 3. Texas—Description and travel—Humor. 4. Texas—Social life and customs—Humor. I. Title.

F391.2.B79   1998   98-37934
976.4—dc21   CIP

Manufactured in the United States of America.

CONTENTS

This book is dedicated to my husband, John Anders:
The best Texan there is.

INTRODUCTION

It's hell living with a woman who's funnier than you are. Particularly when you both write columns for the same newspaper.

But each man must bear his private sorrows with equanimity and dignity.

Now take my wife's book—please.

Herein is a virtual primer for talking the talk and walking the walk, even when the walk is falling-down funny. The shameful fact is, Helen knows us like a book. After 15 years in this state, this woman—a native Virginian—has earned her spurs. In her heart and soul she's as Texan as a bone-in rib eye, a mess of collard greens, and a bowl of black-eyed peas.

Speaking of which, Helen made a rare social gaffe upon first meeting my relatives some years ago. When the conversation turned to food, one of my aunts wanted to know if Helen was partial to peas.

"I love 'em," Helen chimed obligingly.

"What kind in particular, hon?"

"Oh," said Helen, "you know. The green kind . . . *regular* peas."

My family looked blankly at her and fell into silence.

Soon after, I saw to it that my intended became aware of the proud variance of Texas peas.

Today, she can tell a black-eye from a purple hull at ten paces, with or without "snaps." She'll feast on delicate lady cream peas or the hearty big-boy crowder but won't turn her nose up at a mess of field peas or even the humble cow pea. She's been an eager convert. No wonder she's a longtime judge of the Black-Eyed Pea Jamboree in Athens (Texas, not Greece).

She pays honor to all Texas legumes save the under-rated speckled butter bean, and I'm working with her on that.

Helen brings an interloper's eye and reporter's ear to the task of explaining Texas to the rest of the world.

In recent years, she's evolved into my unofficial interpreter when we venture outside the state. She knows I resent the hell out of this, but it's an open question whether I could make myself understood without her. Last year, in New York, I told my bartender it was time to "settle up."

"Saddle up?" howled the bartender, derisively.

"He just needs the check," Helen explained, knowing I would create further confusion if I asked for a "tab." (Helen remembers the time in New York when I requested a "tab" and was brought a diet soft drink—a Tab, as it turned out.)

In an Oregon cafe a few years ago, I consulted the menu and ordered the luncheon special. Our waitress looked at me oddly as I ordered pork loin and rice. I couldn't have spoken the words more plainly.

But Helen had to intercede once again by reordering my meal in English. The waitress jotted down the order and left.

"That's exactly what I said!" I railed.

"No, Baby," Helen soothed, as she patted my hand with condescension. "You told her you wanted the *po-work low-when and r-i-i-i-i-i-i-i-i-i-ce.*"

We Texans have such a talent to amuse.

In London a cockney lass behind the bar strained to understand my call for a glass of "*a-yuhl.*"

Helen spoke up, "Give him an aye-ul."

Miraculously, she had translated Texan to cockney without missing a syllable. In another life, my wife could have worked for the U.N.

After quaffing my ale and walking out of the pub later, I remarked that the Brits weren't nearly so stuffy and rule-happy as I had been led to believe.

"Yes," Helen concurred. "Brittania waives the rules."

You see the problem of living with a simultaneous translator?

As readers of this dead-on volume will doubtless concur, Helen Bryant harbors an undisguised affection for Texans. She even went so far as to up and marry one.

—John Anders

Chapter 1

YOU ARE HERE

And maybe it wasn't your idea.

You got transferred here? Lured by an obscene amount of money? Deposited by an alien vessel?

Whatever. It's *Texas,* not Mars. You can do this.

What you need to do at this point is stop thinking of yourself as a Californian or Oregonian or New Yorker. You are no longer that.

You are a *larval Texan.*

And if you follow the easy steps in this manual, you are fixin' to be, in very little time, a completely formed Texan, indistinguishable from one born here. (In fact, a good first step would be to run out and buy one of those bumper stickers that read "I wasn't born in Texas, but I got here as quick as I could.")

Let's start with some basics:

BIGNESS

Texas is really, really, really, really, really, really big.

It is so big that you can drive all day and not get across it.

It is so big that, on many days, you can get snowed on in Amarillo while your husband is getting sunburned on South Padre Island (though why you'd allow that to happen is beyond me).

It is so big that there are two towns in the state named Jumbo. And three named Punkin Center. And six named Lone Star. And eight named Friendship. And fourteen named Fairview. And *eighteen* named Midway, though only one is big enough to have its own post office. (And all of these are far enough away from each other that nobody gets confused—except maybe for the post office if you send a letter to "Midway, Texas" without a zip code.)

Bigness isn't a situation in Texas; it's a religion. Everything is big. Everything *must* be big, from hair to chicken-fried steaks.

Here's how seriously Texas takes its bigness:

The Texas State Capitol building in Austin is taller than the United States Capitol in Washington, D.C. What makes it taller is a statue of a very ugly woman standing on top of the Texas Capitol. She's officially called the Goddess of Liberty, but unofficially, she's known as Old Hatchet Face. Luckily, she's so far up there that you can't see how ugly she really is. (Please don't infer that Texas is big on ugliness. That's not the case. This building is in Austin, where alternative looks are more acceptable than in, say, Dallas—where they'd surely have given her a facelift by now.)

The point is that Old Hatchet Face was placed atop the Texas Capitol specifically to make our capitol taller than the one in Washington, D.C.

It's a bigness thing.

Another example:

There's a statue of Sam Houston off I-45 north of Houston. It's really, really big—67 feet tall. It looks like Sam's about to walk across I-45 and cause a wreck.

In front of the Dallas Zoo, there's a statue of a giraffe. It's really big, too. It has a 40-inch-long tongue snaking out of its mouth and into the sky. Why? So that the giraffe would be taller than the statue of Sam Houston.

Now, no Texan is going to equate Sam Houston with a giraffe. But the giraffe is *bigger*. This was cause for much backslapping over at the Dallas Zoo.

If you're not a tall person, do not despair. You can make up for it with big hair, a big truck, or big talk. More on those later.

THE TEXAS STATE SONG

It's called "Texas, Our Texas," and it's just about as hard to sing as the National Anthem.

The good news: You do not have to learn this song. Nobody knows it. Not all of it, anyway. Here's what you'll need to sing:

Texas, our Texas, all hail the mighty state.
Texas, our Texas . . . . hmmm hmmm hmmm hmmm
hmmm great.
Blah blah blah blah blah, blah blah blah blah blah blah.
Hmmmmmmmm, hmmmmmmm, hmmm, hmmmm,
hmmmm.
God bless you, Texas, hm hm blah blah blah blah.
Blah blah blah blah blah blah blah blah
Throughout the ages long.

It's as simple as that. I guarantee, the born-in-Lubbock parent next to you at the PTA meeting will sing approximately the same thing.

At this point you're saying, "Wait! I thought 'The Yellow Rose of Texas' was the state song!" Nope.

Or perhaps you're saying, "Wait, I thought 'Deep In The Heart of Texas' (clap clap clap clap) was the state song." Nope. But keep clappin' every time you hear it.

Or perhaps you're saying, "Wait! I thought 'The Eyes of Texas' was the state song!" Nope again. And this incorrect assumption has caused more than a few barroom brawls.

"The Eyes of Texas," you see, is the theme song of The University of Texas.

I was enjoying cocktails in California once when the well-intentioned guy at the piano bar, hearing that there was a large group of Texans in the back of the room, began to play and sing "The Eyes of Texas." Those Texans in the back of the room were not pleased and, in fact, began to glare murderously at the singer.

Why? Because these particular revelers had attended Texas A&M University. "The Eyes of Texas" was not their song. Pay attention; this could save your life: People who attend Texas A&M—Aggies, they are called—do not believe that people who attended the University of Texas received a quality education. And people who attend the University of Texas are *certain* that people who attended Texas A&M did not receive a quality education. Rarely will a week pass in which you do not hear an Aggie joke. And, unless you are an Aggie, becoming a Texan will mean telling Aggie jokes. For example:

Did you hear about the Aggie who wouldn't try barbecued beans? He was afraid they'd fall through the holes on the grill.

Then there was this Aggie who was so dumb, his roommate noticed.

You get the idea.

IMPORTANT: Never tell an Aggie joke to an Aggie. He will not find it clever and may decide the occasion merits the opening of a can of Whup-Ass. Chapter 8 (Gettin' Mad and Gettin' Even) will further explain cans of Whup-Ass

5

and occasions that merit their opening. But for now, let's just say that unless you're the one with the can opener, you're not going to enjoy the contents.

So . . . remember that "The Eyes of Texas" should never be played or sung in the presence of Aggies. It is not the state song.

If you hear "The Eyes of Texas" and all you can think of is "I've Been Workin' on the Railroad," turning you into a Texan may take a little longer than I thought.

THE SHAPE OF TEXAS

Texas has a unique shape, and Texans are very proud of it.

It has that nice panhandle on the left side, the top-right section looks like a dog chewed on it, and it has a tail dipping down into Mexico. (You know, of course, that Texas used to be part of Mexico. Had things gone differently, this book would have been entitled *Fixin' to be Mexican*. But they didn't, so it isn't. Still, the penance to be paid for having swiped the state from the Mexicans is that Anglos tend to get very, very sunburned. Use SPF 15. I mean it.)

Take pride in the shape of your new state. The first thing you need to do is install a Texas-shaped hot tub in your back yard (with a fence around it so the dog doesn't fall in). These are plentiful and can accommodate many Texans. They're generally bigger than Colorado-shaped hot tubs, and if you start to feel claustrophobic, you can escape the crowd by floating over to Amarillo.

You can buy Texas-shaped sunglasses, Texas-shaped bricks for your sidewalk, Texas-shaped tortilla chips, Texas-shaped macaroni, and ice trays that make Texas-shaped ice cubes.

Texas-shaped pastries are fairly tricky, but with enough determination, you can make them. I remember one patri-otic Texas woman who made a huge Texas-shaped fruitcake and sent it to the troops during Operation Desert Storm. (I have no statistics on how many of the soldiers were pleased and how many considered this an act of sabotage.)

Cottonwood Valley golf course in Irving has a green shaped like Texas.

If you accidentally grow a Texas-shaped vegetable, or your cow has a spot on it that looks even vaguely like Texas, you must call the local paper immediately.

TEXAS WEATHER

It's hot—except when it's not.

You will find that Texas has very long summers, very short winters, and negligible springs and falls. Around October, you will become very tired of summer and wish that it would go away. Then one morning, you will awaken and it will be 40 degrees outside. All the leaves will have departed the trees overnight and will be sitting in the yard, demanding to be raked.

That was fall.

It will be semi-cold in November and somewhat colder in December, January, and February. (As a Texan, you should begin shivering when the thermometer drops below 40.)

A particularly strong cold wind is known as a *blue norther*. The north is to blame for everything bad that happens in Texas, including getting cold.

And now, we're going to have to talk about the s-word.

No, not snake. SNOW—the substance that strikes terror in the hearts of all Texans. If you live in the Panhandle, you'll be surprised at how much of this stuff you'll see. Think about it: If they'd drawn the lines a little differently, you'd be living in Colorado. It's going to snow on you. Sorry.

If you live in the Dallas-Fort Worth area, it's likely to snow maybe once a year. It might accumulate an inch or less, unless it's an unusual year.

If you live in Houston, San Antonio, or points south, it is not supposed to snow on you at all. If it does, you have cause to weep copiously.

By now, if you are from the north, you are snorting. Snow, especially an inch or so, is no cause for alarm, you say. You are wrong.

When it snows in Minnesota, what happens? They bring out the salt trucks, right? Well, there are no salt trucks in Texas. They do not salt the roads. Snow happens too infrequently for Them (THEM will be used throughout this book to denote people who make decisions whose names we do not know) to want to deal with big piles of salt sitting around. Besides, They're afraid of corroding Their pickup trucks. So, no salt.

They will, if it snows, put *sand* on the roads. This provides traction for the first ten cars that traverse the roadway. After that, it just makes the snow bumpier.

This is why weather forecasters jump up and down and wave their pointy little sticks a lot when snow is forecast. It is time for all of us to get excited.

This is what you do when snow is forecast:

■ Wring your hands.

- Drive immediately to the grocery store and buy vast quantities of everything—water, peanut butter, spray cheese, duct tape. Whatever. You won't need these things. But it's a Texas tradition to gather at the grocery store before it snows.
- Cancel everything you've planned to do for the next week.
- Put your car in the garage if you have one. No, you're not going to be putting on chains or snow tires. Nobody bothers with those here, for the same reason They don't salt the roads.
- Stay glued to the television until you see whether or not it really does snow. If it does, cower in your house and wring your hands until it all melts.

No, do not drive. If you drive, you are going to find two types of drivers on the roads—little old ladies who are moving along at 5 mph, clinging desperately to the wheel, and pickup trucks whizzing along at 70 mph, getting off on all the fish-tailing. (This is their right as truck people, as you will learn in Chapter 5.) Anyone who encounters a slick patch will slam on his or her brakes and go sideways. Into you.

STAY HOME.

What if it's freezing rain instead of snow? Worse. Much worse. Even *you* cannot drive on ice that hasn't been salted. Trust me.

STAY HOME.

And be happy that winter is very short in Texas, your beloved new state.

By March, the warm-up generally has begun—along with the spring monsoon season. Do not live at the low end of a cul-de-sac; it'll be a bayou in the springtime. In

March or April it can rain for weeks and weeks. Or not. It's Texas; it'll do what it wants.

In summer, you will hear the weather forecasters saying things like, "It's really going to cool down tomorrow," and you will be tempted to get all excited. Don't. They mean it'll drop from 110 to about 98.

One thing about Texas: It has tornadoes. Real ones. If you're under a tornado watch, check the radio now and then. If it turns into a tornado *warning*, time to panic. Run into an interior bathroom, jump in the bathtub, and put a mattress over your head.

Why would you do anything so silly?

Because you don't have a basement to hide in. Really. You don't. Go check; I'll wait.

See? No basement. Rarely, rarely does a Texas house have a basement. Texas soil is very shifty and loose. Texas houses often have foundation problems because of shifting and settling. Basements are out of the question. When I first moved to Texas and asked the basement question, I was told that if I had a basement I would wake up one morning and my basement would be two feet to the left of the rest of my house.

So you can't hide in the basement. Conventional wisdom is to head for an interior room, preferably a bathroom with pipes that will help keep the walls intact if it's just an F1 or F2 tornado—the wimps of the tornado world. If an F5 hits your house, you're toast. Relax; the odds of that happening aren't much better than the odds that you'll win the Texas Lottery.

More important than a basement in a Texas house is a garage. That's because it hails a good bit during Texas thunderstorms. Generally, it'll be pea-sized hail. Sometimes it'll be marble-sized. (Occasionally weather forecasters will refer to dime-sized hail, which is really silly: When was the last time you saw flat hail?) But if the hail gets very big, Texas' love for sports kicks in: We have golf ball-size hail. Sometimes we have baseball-sized hail. Either one will make an un-garaged car look like the surface of the moon. As of this writing, we've never seen basketball-sized hail. But this is Texas; don't put it past us.

THE TEXAS LOTTERY

Like many states, Texas has a lottery consisting of a couple of pick-the-numbers games with big jackpots, plus a bunch of scratch-off cards you can buy for a buck apiece. Every now and then you go home with $3 or so.

It is your responsibility as a Texan to play the Texas Lottery at least once a week and make careful plans for how you will distribute the winnings among your family and friends, regardless of the fact that you will not win. You will, at some point, know somebody who knows somebody who wins. But it will not be you.

Perhaps your odds will improve if you pick your numbers while cowering in your bathtub with a mattress over your head.

THE STATE SLOGAN

The state motto is *Friendship*. That's it. Just *Friendship*. Short. Easy to remember. No *Live Free or Die* rhetoric here; just *Friendship*.

And, the fact is, Texans are very friendly. As you become one, you will find that, for no reason at all, you will say "Hi" to people who pass you on the street. Or "Howdy," if you're in cattle country or at the rodeo. Or the universal greeting: "Hot enough for ya?" Between men, a simple nod will often suffice. Women sometimes shriek "Well, hiiiiiiiii!" Don't be alarmed. It's just friendship.

As I pointed out earlier, Texas is big, and many of the roads in it are little two-laners. If you're driving through a rural part of Texas—and you'll need to do that a lot—you're likely to get stuck behind a tractor or a slow-moving brown car. Don't worry. Texas etiquette dictates that the slow-moving vehicle must move over to the shoulder of the road so that you can pass without having to enter the oncoming lane. After you pass, you are to wave to the person who let you pass and say "Thank you," even though you know perfectly well that he can't hear you.

And when it's you who are slower than the guy behind you, you are expected to do likewise—just drive on the shoulder for as long as it takes the guy to get around you. And watch for the wave.

Even as a larval Texan, you may find yourself becoming friendly. You may smile at a waitress in a restaurant. Say "please." Pet a dog that's smiling.

But don't let the situation get out of hand. Remember those signs you see along the highways: *Don't Mess with Texas.* That's not the official motto, but it's the situation.

Some years back, the State Legislature considered a bill to put *The Friendship State* on license plates. The measure was soundly defeated out of fear that the other states would think we were wimps.

So, although friendliness is a part of being Texan, you must be careful not to cross the border into wimpification. Subsequent chapters will deal with how to strike this balance.

THE STATE FLOWER

The state flower is the bluebonnet, and in the spring-time these are all over the place, especially in that part of Central Texas around Austin known as the Hill Country, because it has lots of hills.

Your job as a Texan: Take a drive to see the bluebonnets. Say nice things about the bluebonnets. Do not pick bluebonnets. (It's not technically illegal, but your fellow Texans will frown.)

You may, however, let your kids trample the bluebonnets into oblivion so that you may take their picture cavorting in a field of flowers. And if you are a bride, you may crush as many as necessary to achieve a perfect sitting-in-the-bluebonnets picture.

THE STATE BIRD

It's the mockingbird, but it knows better than to go around doing Ross Perot impressions. It mocks those who deserve to be mocked. It does not tell Aggie jokes.

TEXAS CITIES

A few major facts about a few major places:

Dallas and **Houston** consider themselves the Big Two.

Dallas is sure it is better than Houston. Houston is sure it is better than Dallas. If you live in Dallas, it is your job to disdain Houston. If you live in Houston, you must roll your eyes every time Dallas is mentioned.

You will see no cowboys in Dallas and few in Houston.

Dallas is pronounced "Dall-us" by people who live there and "Dall-is" by people who don't.

This is important: There are no oil wells in Dallas. Not a one. Want to live near an oil well? Move to East Texas— Tyler or Kilgore, for example.

When it comes to good restaurants, Dallas and Houston are both full as ticks. You can eat yourself silly.

Fort Worth is truly where the West begins. Lots of cowboys and men who dress like cowboys. (See Chapter 10: Dressing Texan, to achieve this look if Fort Worth is your new home.) It is a very friendly town, but do not make the mistake of thinking all these friendly people are wimpy. Those boots are made for stompin'.

Arlington is a large—and still growing—city between Forth Worth and Dallas. (If you think of the area as eyeglasses, Fort Worth is an eye, Dallas is an eye and Arlington is the nose.) Fort Worth considers Arlington its suburb. Dallas considers Arlington its suburb. If Arlington is your new home, however, you'd better not refer to it as a suburb of *anything* or your new neighbors will not speak to you.

Plano started life as a suburb too, but it's fixin' to be a big city. It's north of Dallas—sort of a raised eyebrow in the eyeglasses analogy. Lots of important people (Dallas Cowboys, corporate executives and such) live there, so good restaurants have moved in.

Waco, situated on I-35 about halfway between Fort Worth and Austin, is known primarily for being (1) the home of Baylor University and (2) the halfway point when you're driving from Fort Worth to Austin. If you live there, pay no attention to the people who call it "Wacko."

San Antonio is San Antonio. It is not "San Antone," no matter what they say in the movies. It's a huge city and major tourist destination. It's where the Alamo is. Remember the Alamo?

Austin is the state capital, the home of the University of Texas, and the new electronics hotbed. It has bigtime traffic problems, but everybody in Austin is so laid back that they don't really care, man. Pass the tofu.

Amarillo is famous mainly for two reasons: (1) Oprah Winfrey went to court there to defend herself against charges that she libeled a hamburger. (That a Texas jury could sit straight-faced and consider this issue should tell you something about how seriously this state takes its cows.) (2) It rhymes with "pillow" and thus has been in a lot of country songs.

SMALL TOWNS

Texans have a good time naming their towns.

You can live in Beans, Blanket, Blowout, Bootleg, Bug Tussle, Ben Hur, Dimple, Fate, Flat Fork, Fly Gap, Golly, Good Neighbor, Grit, Hail, Impact, Jolly, Lollipop, Magnet, Monkeyville, Noodle, Noonday, Oatmeal, Odds, Pancake, Pep, Poetry, Ponder, Rabbit Hollow, Raccoon Bend, Razor, Scissors, Scurry, Stranger, Sublime, Telephone, Tool, or Tuxedo.

Or Uz.

If you set up housekeeping in Frog and decide you don't like it, you can move to Frognot.

To be sure, many of these are just little unincorporated bends in the road, but they had enough people there (say, 10) to get the state to put up a sign. That makes 'em legit.

If you're the aggressive sort, you might choose to live in Cut And Shoot, Gun Barrel City, Point Blank, Gunsight, Battle, Bivoac Estates, Draw, Dies, Scrappin Valley, or Eulogy.

If all that scares the heck out of you, move to Security.

You have to wonder about the town meetings that resulted in some of these names. Some are easy to figure. Hail, for example.

But imagine the process that led one small dot in the road to be named Jot-Em-Down.

"What we gonna name this town, Bubba?"

"I dunno, R.Q. Got any ideas?"

"A few maybe."

"Well, jot 'em down."

"Hey, Bubba, that's a great idea! We'll call our town Jot-Em-Down!"

There's a town in the wilds of West Texas called Halfway, and I can't see that it's halfway to anything. But if you live in Muleshoe and you're headed for Halfway, when you get to Earth you'll be almost halfway to Halfway.

You can live in Earth, sure. Or you can live in Mars, Venus, Mercury, Saturn, or Pluto. You're out of luck if you had your heart set on Neptune, Jupiter, or Uranus—nobody's picked those names. Yet. (There's no Yet yet either, for that matter.)

There's a fairly well-known Texas town named Paris, and if you're planning a trip to Paris you need to specify, "the one in France," or people will automatically assume you mean the Texas one. Same with Athens.

If you're into body parts, you can settle down in Elbow, Foot, Back, or Babyhead.

An optimistic sort? Try Serene Hills, Content, or Climax.

I imagine that life in Moonshine Colony is a lot more fun than in Dull.

Might want to steer clear of Looneyville.

On the other hand, you shouldn't read too much into the name of a town.

The town of West, Texas, is not in West Texas. It is in Central Texas. And Desert is in North Texas, where the biggest stretch of sand is likely to be your cat box.

The town of Whiteface is not racist; it was named that because of white-faced Hereford cows.

Only a handful of people live in Lotta. There are blatant heterosexuals residing in Gay Hill. People in Placid have been known to get riled. And there are times when the folks in Uncertain have been known to move with great resolve.

My personal favorite: Ding Dong. It's in Bell County.

WINTER TEXANS

Perhaps you're only a part-time Texan. You maintain a home in another part of the country, but when it gets cold in that part of the country you like to be somewhere warmer. So you become a Winter Texan, also known as a Snowbird. (Pay no attention to the locals who say Iowa stands for Idiots Out Walking Around. They are happy to be getting your dollars.)

You're probably wintering in Far East Texas or, more likely, Far South Texas—the Rio Grande Valley, perhaps South Padre Island.

Here are the rules for being a Winter Texan:

- You will wear a brightly colored jogging suit at all times. You don't have to jog; just wear the suit.
- If you have been dyeing your hair, you will stop. Let it go gray. Men, go for a mid-length, tousled look. Consider a beard and/or mustache. Women, have your hair cut into the shape of an inverted bowl. Beards and mustaches are optional. The key here is to keep your looks low-maintenance. You haven't come this far in life to spend your leisure time trying to appear as though you just stepped out of *Vogue*. The humidity is going to make you look ratty anyway.

■   Buy a big ol' motor home. The bigger the better.

That's all it takes. Y'all come on down. The more the merrier.

TEXAS ROADS

. . . are always under construction.

Chapter 2

YO, BUBBA!

Becoming a Texan gives you the perfect opportunity to dump—or alter—a name that you don't like.

Why do you think there are so many people in Texas named Bubba or Tex or Bo or Buster? Because they were born Lawrence or Walter or Clarence. Texas is a state in which your name is a reflection of your true self—or maybe what you'd like that self to be.

There is, of course, nothing inherently wrong with the name Walter. But it is not a very Texan name. By the time you finish this chapter, you'll have several ideas on how to improve upon it.

Texans are fearless people, and they're not afraid to choose colorful names. Thus, a long time ago, a Texas governor named James Hogg hauled off and named his daughter Ima.

Ima Hogg. It's not legend; it's truth. What's legend—and entirely untrue—is that she had a sister named Ura. (This legend falls under Texas Tall Tale Telling, which will be addressed in Chapter 3. You, too, can fashion fiction about your sister's name if you so choose.)

There are names that would be considered flamboyant in other states that just seem to work in Texas. Angus, for example. You might look at somebody funny in Chicago if his name was Angus. But in Texas, Angus works. Maybe because it's a kind of cow.

Shoot, Texas is probably the only state that could actually have kids named Pebbles and Bam-Bam. The truth: I know a Dallas woman named Pebble. I don't know a Bam-Bam—but it could happen! I do know a man named Boo. That is his legal name. He didn't start out as a Boo, but he had his name changed to that. He is a brave Texan.

MEN'S NAMES

In some cases, names just happen to you in Texas.

If you're redheaded, for example, your name is Red. That's it. End of discussion.

If you're short, you're Shorty. If you're tall, you're also Shorty. (Texas irony rears its head.) That's unless you're both tall and massive, in which case you have the option of being named Bigun.

If you have an out-of-control mustache, you're probably going to be Brushy. You don't like the name? Shave the mustache.

Actor Rip Torn, a native Texan, once told me had no choice about being called Rip. His mother named him Elmore, so it's just as well.

"If you were a Torn and a male," he said, "you were Rip." So there were a lot of Rips in Rip's family, including an uncle who somehow earned the title Big Rip.

Here are some other circumstances under which you have no choice:

Your last name	Your new first name
Peterson	Pete
Anderson	Andy
Thompson	Tommy
Warner	Pop
Brown	Buster
Anything starting with "Gos"	Goose

If your last time is Smith and you like the name "Smitty," you can be that. But it's not mandatory in this state.

If your name doesn't fall into one of those categories, you have a voice in what you will be called. Some options:

1. Pick up on a physical feature or favorite thing.

Let's say you like to play the drums. You might call yourself Sticks. Got big ears? Try Lobes.

You like watching the bats fly out from under the bridge in Austin? Maybe you should be Bat. (That name would also work if you're a big Bat Masterson fan.)

My husband's high school nickname, which his longtime friends still some- times use, was Okra. The guy liked okra. Two of his friends also liked okra, and they were named Okra as well. Among themselves, they often abbreviated the name, so that a chance meeting on campus resulted in the following exchange:

"Oke!"

"Oke!"

"Oke!"

"Oke!"

"Oke!"

"Oke!"

Talking about your meaningful student dialogue.

So, let's say for the sake of this chapter's argument that your name is Walter. Let's think about some Texas names you could fashion in this fashion:

You could be Beans because you're an accountant (bean counter), Frisco because you're from San Francisco (yes, I know nobody in San Francisco calls it that, but it still makes a cool name) or Docks because you wear Dockers all the time. One thing's for sure: After you've had this kind of name for a really long time, nobody will remember how you got it. So heck, pick a name out of thin air and get your wife to start calling you that. It'll catch on.

2. Use your initials.

Many Texans go by their initials: L.D., R.Q., C.F. or whatever. And you can be pretty sure that those guys' real names aren't as cool as their initials. The tough dude you know as A.P. Clark could well be Aloysius Poindexter Clark.

Try your own initials out for size.

Some combinations would seem to be a bad idea, but that doesn't always keep Texas men from using them. My husband was once advised there was a guy named I.P.

Rainwater somewhere in the state. Certain this was a joke, he checked—and learned that I.P. exists!

But if you don't like the way your initials sound, you don't necessarily have to use your real ones.

My husband has a longtime friend named O.T. For years he thought those were the guy's real initials. Turns out they're not. And no, his name has nothing to do with overtime. It's just that when he was younger, he was extremely obnoxious. Everyone called him Obnoxious Tom. It was eventually shortened to O.T.

So, Walter, if your middle initial is, for example, C., and you don't want to be thought of as a water closet, fashion yourself an image as Travelin' Walter. That way, you can be T.W.

3. Attach Bob to your name.

This is easy. You're James? Become Jim Bob. You can be Jerry Bob or Johnny Bob or Harry Bob or Tom Bob.

There are, of course, some names that do not work with Bob. Richard is one. Richard Bob sounds dumb. Richie Bob will make your neighbors' eyes roll. Same with Ricky Bob or Rick Bob. And don't even *think* of being Dick Bob (although your Aggie friends might like it because it would take the joke pressure off them). If your name is Richard, use one of the other options in this chapter.

Now you, Walter: You're going to have to do a little alteration on this concept. Walter Bob will not do. Wally Bob, on the other hand, will do very nicely.

4. Use both your names.

This works especially well if you are a Joe Frank or a Robert Earl or some other combination of relatively short names. Horace Algernon is not a combination that works very well. Actually, there's not much of anything you can do with Horace Algernon except go back to using initials. HA!

Two groups that most often use the double-name ploys are country musicians and serial killers. But you don't *have* to be one of those. Just thought I'd throw that in.

5. Use a variation on your last name.

Perhaps your name is Oliver Twist. You could be Twist or Twister. The latter is an especially good Texas name in view of the weather situation, and it implies wonderful things about your disposition.

I must emphasize: The name has to work with your personality. I have a writer friend whose name is Mike Shropshire. He is not a Mike; he is a Shrop. Even his wife calls him Shrop. His tombstone will someday say Shrop. A Mike is a very serious person. A Shrop is a wild-eyed tale-spinner.

What's your last name, Walter? If it's McElroy, you can be Mack. If it's Buckingham, you could be Buck. You get the idea.

A last name can be a gold mine of opportunities. Unless your name is Buttafucco.

6. Use one of the stock Texas names.

The state can always use another Bubba. If you qualify.

And that's the catch: If you're going to choose the name Bubba, you're going to have to live up to it. You can't be Bubba and never cross the street unless the little "Walk" light is on. You can't be Bubba and order the chicken Caesar salad for lunch. You can't be Bubba and drive a Cadillac Seville.

You have an image to uphold if you are Bubba. You must be Super Texan. Tell you what: Finish reading this book and see how much of a Texan you can make yourself. Then decide whether or not you can be Bubba.

If not, there are other stock Texas names that carry a less heavy burden of proof. You might become Bum (you don't have to be one to be named that), Buster, Jock, Butch, Bud, Coy, Gus, Hank, or Billy Bob.

So, Walter, you see that you have a choice. You can be T.W. or Wally Bob or maybe even Bubba—if you decide you qualify. One thing's for sure: A Walter by any other name will sound far, far more like a Texan.

FEMALE NAMES

Ladies, you don't need to be afraid of interesting names either. In fact, you can name yourself just about anything under the sun, and it will fly in this state.

Sure, Ima Hogg is the extreme.

But please consider that there are, at this moment, actual people walking around in the great state of Texas with the names Twinkle, Muffin, Brooksie, Honey, and Silky. So if you want to call yourself Banana Cream Pie, go for it.

The general rule is that the wealthier you are, the sillier the name you can have. A Teensie will, in general, be much richer than a Brenda.

If you're not one of the society set and don't really want to be a Cupcake, Fluffy, or a Lambie, there are options.

You can do initials, just like the guys. It doesn't happen much, but I do know of one woman called J.R. And some people call me H.B. (When the alternative abbreviation is "Hel," I'm grateful for H.B.)

The female equivalent of Bubba is, of course, Sissy—Bubba being derived from *brother*. But Sissy does not carry the burden that Bubba does. You don't have to be Super Texan to be a Sissy. For that matter, you don't have to be a sissy to be Sissy.

And by the way, if you are indeed somebody's sister and want to call yourself Sister, you can do that, too. That's true in the South, and it's true in Texas.

Attaching Bob to your name is not an option. Sorry.

But you *can* do the double-name thing: Betty Sue or Ruth Ann or Annie June or—if you have a *whole* lot of money—Fluffy Star.

Or, you can marry yourself into a cool name.

Lida Light marries Frank Blue—she's Lida Light Blue. Pretty cool. (Lida, by the name, is a charming Texas female name. There are lots of Lidas in Texas.)

In Texas, you still have the option of forgetting about your name altogether and using your husband's. You can identify yourself solely as "Mrs. Frank Albertson." Heck, people don't even have to know you *have* a name.

This might be the way to go if your name is Hortense.

Chapter 3

TALKIN' THE TALK

Now, we're fixin' to talk about talkin'. And the first thing we'd better get straight is that talkin' Texan and talkin' Southern are two different things. Let's take a very basic sentence:

Pass the bread.

In Southern, this is: *Pa-yis thu buh-re-yid.*

In Texan, it's: *Pais thu breeed.*

They're two different ways of talkin', and although the two share some crucial words—particularly *y'all*—they're not the same, no matter what Hollywood seems to think. Neither the Southern nor the Texas speech pattern is lazy. Both require hard work. A Southerner has to make as many syllables as possible out of each word. A Texan may add syllables to certain words, but in general the idea is to stretch vowels to the limit. Ideally, the word *bred* should last about three seconds—long enough for it to cool down enough to eat.

Y'ALL

Texans, like Southerners, realize that when the English language was invented, its inventors forgot to come up with a second person plural. That is the purpose served by *y'all*.

Important: *Y'all* is **always** plural. If you refer to one person as *y'all*, you will immediately mark yourself as somebody Not From Around Here.

It's this way:

Singular	*Plural*
I go	*We go*
You go	*Y'all go*
He goes	*They go*

And get this: Texan even has a plural of *y'all—all y'all*. Conjugate the super-plural this way:

> *We all go*
> *All y'all go*
> *All 'em go*

This form is generally used as an emphatic.

Regular second-person plural: *Y'all are going to the meeting.*

Second person super-plural: *I expect **all y'all** to go to the meeting.*

The implication: You'd all better be there.

All 'em, the third person super-plural, makes emphatically clear that the speaker is referring to *all* the people or things in a group. It is often accompanied by a wave of the hand in the direction of what is being referred to:

All 'em's my cows.

FIXIN' TO

Only in Texas can you fix something that ain't broke. "Fixin' to" is the first word combination a Texan child learns, so it may as well be the first one *you* learn.

It is a truly effective verb. To wit:

"Frankie, have you cleaned up your room yet?"

"No, but I'm fixin' to."

"Oh. OK."

Those two words—*"fixin' to"*—imply that the person, although not engaged in the task in question, is making preparations to begin the task. *Fixin'* is an active word. It is more reassuring than "I will" or "I plan to."

OL'

You should be aware that when a Texan talks about a *big ol' sandwich* or a *li'l ol' dog,* he is not making a statement about the age of the sandwich or the dog. The word *ol'* is just a grace note of the language. Which is more interesting? *Big sandwich* or *big ol' sandwich*? There you go. Practice using the word *ol'*:

What do you get into each night? That's right: Your good ol' bed.

For that matter, you yourself are a good ol' boy or good ol' girl. It doesn't mean you're old. It means you're good.

MESS

There are three kinds of messes in Texas:

- The verb *to mess with,* meaning to antagonize: As in, *Don't mess with Texas* or *Don't mess with me.*
- The collective noun *mess,* meaning a whole lot: As in, *I'm gonna cook me a mess of greens.*
- The noun *mess,* referring to someone who's a bit loony or outrageous: As in, *Your kids are a mess!* (When somebody says this about your children, the correct response is to chuckle and shake your head. It does not mean that your children are ill groomed. It simply means that they wisecrack, show off, and otherwise attract a lot of attention. If, however, they are still *a mess* when they're 40 years old, there's a problem.)

SIR AND MA'AM

Here's another crossover with the South. Children are taught to call their elders "Sir" and "Ma'am." It's out of respect, not subservience. I've had many a northerner complain to me about the practice, but I always thought it was wonderful—up until the first time a young man I was interviewing for a job called me "ma'am." Then I realized I was considered an elder. I was, at the time, thirty-two. This bothered me to the point where I told the young man, who was highly qualified for the job, that he would have no consideration for the position until he quit calling me "ma'am."

Still, it's supposed to be a sign of respect. Keep that in mind when you hear the kids (thirty-year-old kids included) call you that.

YEEHA AND YAHOO

These are not interchangeable.

What you say when you're really excited is "Yeeha," sometimes spelled "yee-ha." Either is acceptable.

Use the word copiously when you attend a rodeo or musical event. Throwing you hat in the air while you yell it is a nice touch, so long as you are good at catching it.

The word "yahoo" is used in only two contexts:

- In reference to the soft drink Mountain Dew and
- In reference to somebody from the northern portions of the country who comes down here thinking he knows a whole lot but who doesn't even know the difference between "yeeha" and "yahoo." That makes him the latter.

GETTING THE
ACCENT RIGHT

Like I said, it's not the same as talking Southern.

Southern emphasizes making everything into as many syllables as possible, whereas Texan merely draws those vowels out to their maximum capacity.

And the big kahuna of all vowels is the *i*. The *i*'s have it. Anytime a Texan runs across an *i* in conversation, he makes the most of it.

You look real *niiiiiiiiiiiiice.*

I'd like some *riiiiiiiiiiiiice.* (The waitress will wish you'd just order a baked potato and be done with it.)

Just draw that sucker out till you run out of air.

It's a beautiful *niiiiiiiiiiiiiiiiiiiiiiiiiiiiight.*

It's a very flat *i* you want, too. It's not *noight* or *nait.* Just *nite*—but throw in a lot of extra *i*'s, of course. The vowel is so flat, it's almost pronounced as an *a*. There's very little difference between *night* and *gnat* in Texas pronunciation. Context is the only clue. There's no such thing as a good gnat, so the guy must be bidding you farewell.

This pronunciation thing can cause a lot of problems.

Make sure you're careful when you ask for a piece of ice, for example.

A friend of mine once called to place a classified ad for a couple of Wet Bikes—a Wet Bike being a brand name of a personal watercraft.

"Tell me how you want the ad to read," said the person at the newspaper.

"For sale: Two Wet Bikes."

"Sir!" exclaimed the classified-taker. "We cannot and will not say that in our newspaper!"

My friend was confused until he realized the person on the other end of the phone did not understand what he was saying. She thought he was using a derogatory term for someone who has crossed the Rio Grande without permission.

Another tricky vowel is the long *a*. It rambles around into almost a long *i* at the end. Thus, the word *play* sounds like *ply,* except that the vowel is extended for a few seconds.

Practice saying the following sentence:

My friend Clay is from Waco.

It should sound this way: *My friend Clyyy is from Wyyyco.*

My husband was once in need of a glass of wine in another part of the country.

"Do you have a chardonnay?" he asked.

The bartender blanched: "Do I have a sharp knife!?"

Because of these vowel irregularities, it's important for larval Texans to speak clearly and distinctly to longtime Texans to avoid being misunderstood.

Another classified ad story:

A classified in a Texas paper read: *Lost: Egyptian bass boat.*

Egyptian bass boat? Do they fish for bass in Egypt? And how do you go about losing a bass boat, anyway?

A couple of days later, the corrected ad ran: *Lost: Egyptian passport.*

Oh.

I can only assume that the man dictating the ad was from Egypt, and he was misunderstood by the Texan ad-taker, who may not have traveled much but who sure knew the importance of a bass boat.

So speak Texan carefully, and carry a big stick, so that if anybody laughs at your accent you can open a can of Whup-Ass on him.

Short *e*'s in Texan are pronounced like they are everywhere else, but for longer duration: *Breeeeeeeed.* There are certain parts of Texas, notably East Texas (it's close to the South, you see) that add a syllable and make it *bre-yid.* But generally it's just bred.

An *e* does something different, though, when it's attached to a *g*.

Leg is *laig.* A hen lays an *aig.*

Other than that, vowels are pretty much the same as they are all over. Just longer, is all.

IS ALL

This is just a way to end a sentence, is all.

AND STUFF

This is another way to end a sentence if it is a sentence listing more than one thing. Use this if you feel the list should be longer than it is, but you just can't think of any other things to put on the list:

We were just talkin' and drinkin' and stuff.

She's just real pretty and nice and stuff.

PESKY PLACES

Watch your pronunciation on the following Texas places:

Fort Worth: *FOAT Wuth*

Bexar County: *Bear County*

Gruene: *Green*

Mexia: *Muh-HAY-uh*

Waxahachie: *Woks-a-hatch-ee*

Balch Springs: *Box springs*

Refugio: *Ree-fury-oh*

COLORFUL TEXAS VERBIAGE

Texans are known for their colorful expressions.

Former Texas governor Ann Richards, when she's at a public event, likes to say, "I haven't had so much fun since a pig ate my brother."

Now, a pig never ate Ann's brother. We all know that. But all of us who have a brother know how much fun it would be to see a pig eat him, so we just love this expression.

Bert Shipp, a Dallas television newsman, likes this one: "There's no back door to that Alamo." That means you may as well forget about it, because whatever situation you're in, you're going to lose. Not just lose, die. You are sunk, pard. You have dug you a hole you ain't never gettin' out of. You get the idea . . . .

Try making up a colorful phrase of your own. Choose something with which you have a familiarity, such as pigs or the Alamo in the examples above. Craft a sentence around it. Get your whole family involved. Then try it out on a Texan. He'll either love you or shoot you.

TEXAS LANGUAGE

There are some words that are peculiar to Texas. Whole books have been written on this subject, so I'll just define some that are particularly peculiar and open to misinterpretation:

Tump   A combination of *tip* and *dump,* as in: *Dang, Mildred, my ice tea tumped over.*

Tank   A pond, generally created to feed livestock. Sometimes called a stock pond. But you'll be pleased to know that "getting tanked" means the same thing in Texas as it does anywhere else.

Bobwar   Barbed wire. The stuff that keeps the cows from wandering around all over the road. Usually.

Yawn yoan   "You're on your own." This is the exception to the rule that we Texans always drawl everything out and make it longer. This is a two-syllable dismissal, to be used in such circumstances as this:

"I think I'll go beat up that big guy in the corner of the room."

"Yawn yoan."

Yawn yoan immediately absolves the speaker of any involvement in whatever is about to come down.

Awl biness   Oil business. It's a bit of an abbreviation, because the awl biness has been a bit abbreviated in Texas for a good many years. It used to make everybody rich. Then oil prices deflated, folks stopped drilling, and the awl biness isn't awl it used to be. So when you're introduced to somebody and he says he's in the awl biness, that could mean he made a fortune, which he still has. Or it may mean he's busted and will try to separate you from what few hard-earned bucks you have. You've been warned.

Pissant   It refers to a small black ant, as opposed to a fire ant (see Chapter 11). But in general, it means anything insignificant: *I'm sick of this pissant job.*

Bigass   Big. The -ass suffix just makes it seem bigger: *That is one bigass truck.*

Passel   A whole lot.

Rat cheer   Gimme an M! Gimme an I! Just kidding. It means "right here," as in: *Sit rat cheer and I'll tell you a story.*

Longneck   Not a giraffe, no. A beer in a glass bottle with a long neck. The Lone Star longneck is the official beer of Texas.

Bass ackwards   Has nothing to do with bass. It means ass backwards but sounds more acceptable.

Ranch   Pronounced *rainch*. (1) A spread for the raising of livestock. In many states, a "ranch" can refer to any one-story house. This is not the case in Texas, and if you refer to your Plano tract home as a ranch, you will be laughed at all the way to Alpine. (2) The favorite salad dressing in Texas. It's the house dressing in many restaurants.

Tard   Exhausted.

Dog tard   Extremely exhausted.

Coke   Generic word for all forms of soda pop. "I want a Coke," your friend will say, to which you will reply: "What kind?"

Carry   Means take, as in *I'll carry you to your car in my truck*. You don't have to physically lift the person.

Dang   Swear word acceptable to just about everybody.

Boy hidy   An affirmation:

"Hot one, ain't it?"

"Boy hidy!"

Checkin' ma tires   This is what a male does when he pulls over to the side of the road for no apparent reason. He has a reason all right, and it's generally that it's a long way between towns and he's been consuming large quantities of liquid.

Riled   Mad, as in angry.

Full as a tick   No longer hungry. I will warn you that a lot of mamas don't much like this expression.

Snatch you bald   What mamas threaten to do to kids who are ill mannered enough to say "full as a tick."

The whole enchilada   Everything, and it usually doesn't mean food. *I thought my ex-wife was gonna settle for half my money, but she wanted the whole enchilada.*

COLLEGE TALK

Gig 'em, Aggies!   This is the catchphrase of Texas A&M University and is applied to all opponents. Gigging a frog refers to spearing it with a sharp stick, so this is no doubt the effect intended here.

Hook 'em, Horns!   The equivalent for the University of Texas. This shout is generally accompanied by the official UT gesture, which consists of a closed fist with the index finger and pinkie extended, forming "horns." The uninitiated often are taken aback to see cute young girls making this gesture, but upon close examination, you will see that it is harmless.

VISITING

In many parts of the country, "to visit" means to go to somebody else's house. That is not what it means in Texas. In Texas, visiting is just sitting around talking. And if there's no place to sit, it means standing around and talking.

While the Immigration and Naturalization Service was tearing down our van, we all just visited.

This does not mean that during this time you took off for nearby houses to say "hi." It means you just stood there by your van, while it was being disassembled, talking to each other. It also implies that you were not nervous, so the INS probably gave you your van back without finding anything. *Visiting* is polite, noncontroversial conversation. It is in no way stressful, except when you've done it with houseguests for more than five days in a row.

TEXAS TALL TALES

It's the bigness thing again. No matter what happens to a Texan, he can big it up into a more impressive story.

This is an art form with many names.

One expert practitioner—a Canadian-native broadcaster named Alex Burton, who is now so thoroughly Texan that he's often quoted by out-of-staters as the quintessential Bubba—calls it Texas hoo-rah.

It's also known as hokum or malarkey.

But mostly, it's known as good ol' Texas *bool-sheet*.

I know that isn't a word a lot of you incorporate into your daily lives. But it's really a very big part of Texas talkin', and I would be remiss if I didn't bring it up and explain what it really is. Try to bear with me. It won't take long.

Bool-sheet refers to something that is less than true. That separates it from *chicken-sheet* (cowardly), *horse-sheet* (worthless) and *ape-sheet* (crazy).

What you have to keep in mind is that in Texas, *bool-sheet* is not necessarily an awful thing.

If you've been to a Texas country-western bar, you've already noticed the glee with which people shout "Bool-sheet!" at a predetermined time during the dancing of the Cotton-Eyed Joe. They're not mad at anybody. Nobody has done any lying during the dance. It's just something people yell while they're doing that dance. It makes them happy. After you've done the dance a few times, you'll be happy too. (Grab a longneck; it'll help.)

Good bool-sheet is actually admired in Texas.

"I caught a bass that was three feet long day before yesterday," you will declare.

"Bool-sheet!" your friend will reply. But he'll be *smiling with admiration* when he says it.

The bad kind of bool-sheet involves lies that have an impact on somebody else.

"You've owed me that money for six months, R.D."

"I know, I know, and I was gonna pay you last week, but my wife went and spent the money I'd saved up."

"Bool-sheet."

"And I'm gonna pay you this Friday because I have a sure-fire system that's gonna win me the lottery."

"Bool-sheet!"

And when Friday rolls around and you haven't won the lottery, you had better not be spreading any more of that commodity or a can of Whup-Ass might be opened.

But as long as it doesn't hurt anybody, a little exaggeration is considered recreational, and its purveyors are considered heroes.

The basic rule: It has to evolve from a germ of truth. It cannot be whole-cloth lie. It must be woven from a strand of something that actually happened.

Thus, you might tell a tale about being attacked by a big ol' bunch of snakes. The essence of truth is that you saw a snake. In the road. While you were in your car. But over time, the car gets lost, the number of snakes multiplies, and they get real aggressive.

Or, let's take this statement: *All 'em's my cows.*

Maybe they are. Maybe they aren't. 'Em's cows; that's for sure. But who's to say whose they are, unless you happen to be talking to the guy who really owns them?

If you fix your eyes steady enough, people are likely to buy it, and you will have become a proud purveyor of the Texas tall tale . . . or whatever you choose to call it.

It is hoped that by the time you get around to trying your hand at this, you will have learned how to talk Texan well enough to make your story fly.

If not, well . . . *yawn yoan.*

Chapter 4

WALKIN' THE WALK

Slow down. This is Texas.

Unless you are being chased, you generally have two options:

You can amble or you can mosey.

An amble is a slow walk with a light to moderate arm swing. Moseying is about as aimless a gait as there is. You don't have to swing your arms. You don't even have to go in any particular direction. You just mosey along as you see fit. You may get there; you may not.

Either the mosey or the amble may be used to get from Point A to Point B, the real point being that there is no rush.

There are a few other gaits suitable for special occasions:

- **The lumber.** You may lumber if you are large and tired. An arm swing is a nice touch.
- **The ease.** You may *ease* on down the road, or on over to your girlfriend's house, or anywhere you need to be. Use of this word affords you the option of using the

amble or the mosey or even the lumber, as long as you do it with no sense of urgency.

■ **The beer-carrying trudge.** This is a special sort of amble for use when you have a beer in your hand. Hold the beer at chest level, extend your belly and lean back just a bit, providing a counterbalance for your beer. Now, slide your feet along so as not to spill. Do not swing your arms. Do not bob your head. Only your legs should move—sort of like one of those Irish dancers, only much slower and with a beer.

- **The stagger.** After you've been doing the beer-carrying trudge all day long, you will find that it has evolved into the stagger. At this point, it is unwise to carry around the beer. Drink it sitting still, or just go to bed.
- **The bowlegged swagger.** This is a cowboy gait, earned by those who have been on horses long enough to have legs shaped like parentheses. The gait emphasizes moving side to side as you move forward. Lead with your chest.

THE DALLAS EXCEPTION

You are allowed to move faster than a mosey or amble in Dallas, even if you are not being chased. And OK, you can move fast in Houston, too.

The simple fact is that if you don't scramble a bit in these two cities, you're likely to get stepped on or run over. For the same reason you have to talk fast in these two cities, you have to walk fast: There is a great deal of nervosity in the cities. Besides, some of these people are, in fact, being chased—by the IRS.

There are various gaits you may use for moving quickly:

- **The skeedaddle.** To be used if there is someplace you must leave in a big hurry.
- **The vamoose.** This is probably derived from the Spanish *vamos,* which means "we go." But vamoose means we go *very very fast.*
- **The haul ass.** There is a degree of urgency with this one.
- **The cut 'n' run.** The gait of last resort, to be used when you are being chased by somebody—or some*thing*—mighty fearsome.

RUNNING THE RUN

Are you a runner? Confess.

Optional running is frowned upon in most parts of Texas. Remember: It's hot. Nobody in his right mind runs during the months of May through September. You are likely to drop dead outright if you do.

Also, if people see you running they will often (a) stop you to ask for directions to something you know nothing about or (b) try to hit you with their trucks.

If you must engage in optional running, use a sidewalk.

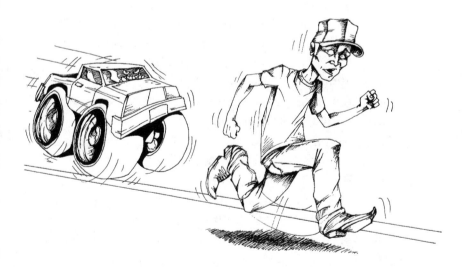

TEXAS DIRECTIONS

Let's say you and your fellow larval Texans are just taking a little mosey down the road, when you become thirsty. You spot a fellow Texan to ask directions to a place to get a Dr Pepper, the soft drink of choice (because it's made here).

Do not expect him to talk about street names. He will tell you to go "down the road mile, mile and a half" or go "a fur piece to your right" or "take a little jog to the right," which does not mean to run a quarter mile. It means the road curves to the right, but only slightly. You may continue to amble through this jog.

He might also tell you to "go left at the first red light." In giving directions, Texans refer to all lights as red. They might be green when you get there. Thus, if you are told "go right at the fourth red light," go right at the fourth light, whether or not it is red.

Although you cannot expect to be given street names, you *will* be given points of reference:

"It's about a mile past the Wally-Mart, right beside the Texaco and across from the Mickey D's. If you get to the Monkey Ward's, you've gone too far."

"You'll see a big blue dog on the porch and my truck parked in the front yard." (You may assume at this point that the dog and the truck don't move much. And you may be right.)

If you find these sorts of directions confusing, just smile and say "thankya" and ease on down the road in the general direction in which you've been pointed. Then ask again in a couple of blocks. You'll get entirely different directions.

WHERE TO GO

A true Texan never lets anybody tell him where to go, but we will make an exception here because you are new to the state.

Here are some excellent places to try out your new Texas walk:

- Walk to the nearest gas station. Buy yourself a Dr Pepper and a bag of Fritos and walk home.
- Walk down the beach if you happen to be near one.
- Walk to where your cows are.
- If you're in San Antonio, walk on the River Walk. Just once. Because after you have been here long enough to become a fully formed Texan, you will not go there again. The River Walk is for tourists.
- If you're in Austin, walk on Sixth Street. Enjoy the tattoo parade.
- If you're in Dallas and Houston, be advised that you can't walk *to* anything. Both cities are very spread out, and wherever you want to be is going to be far from where you are.
- If it's raining, heck, just walk to the refrigerator, get a beer, and practice the beer-carrying trudge.
- Walk to your truck. Get in. Now drive somewhere.

DANCIN' THE DANCE

Now that you've learned to walk the walk, it is time to learn to dance the dance.

Texas dancing is known as boot-scootin'. And that's generally what you do. Like any dancing, boot-scootin' has many variations, combinations, and permutations, and if you really get into this you'll get to where you twirl around, your partner twirls around, you do a lot of fancy stuff with your feet, and you're all over the dance floor at once.

But at the beginning, you're just going to trudge slowly across the floor—the guy forward, the girl backward—to get the hang of it.

The major Texas dance is the two-step. This is essentially a shuffling fox-trot type thing. Just about any country-western bar can teach it to you in about 20 minutes, so there's no need to go drawing a bunch of little feet here to show you how. Once you learn the two-step, any dance floor in the state is yours.

The major Texas group dance is the Cotton-Eyed Joe. A specific Cotton-Eyed Joe song is played to dance this one to. Everybody partners up in a circle and does some scootin' and leg crossin' and yellin'. You don't even have to take lessons. This one's easy. Just watch it once, then join in the next time. Warning: This dance goes both forward and backward, and it is a big disgrace to go the wrong way. It ruins the whole dance for everybody, and you will have to go home.

Line dancing has become a big deal for Texas women, since it involves a good bit of hip work, turns, and head tossing. Arms are often tucked behind the hips. It's show-off material. Most Texan men don't really like tucking their arms behind them and waving their butts around in a line dance. If you are a man and you like line dancing, be fore-warned: Don't advertise what you don't intend to use.

Then there's the ubiquitous dance that might be called Just Walkin' Around. You and your partner just hang on to each other and sway back and forth. You don't really go anywhere. You can do this to songs like Willie Nelson's "Blue Eyes Cryin' in the Rain." The dance is low-impact, it affords you the opportunity to get close to your partner and try out some belly-rubbin', and the two of you can hold each other up if it's been a long night.

Once you are through dancing, you can amble on home. Right.

Let's be reasonable. Home is too far to walk. What you need is a *truck!*

Proceed to the next chapter, please.

Chapter 5

YOUR TRUCK

Never mind that you have nothing to pick up. You have to have a pickup.

Why? Several reasons:

- In a truck, you sit high in the saddle. You can see over everybody else in traffic. You can *look down* on everybody else. You know where the traffic jams are, so that

you can find a slightly illegal way of getting around
them. You know when the exit's coming up. You know
everything. You have a high profile. Life is good.

■ You're big. Remember the Texas bigness thing. Trucks
are bigger than cars.

■ You *do* have something to haul—ass.

There are more pickup trucks in Texas than in any
other state in the union. That's because the good people of
this state are wise. They know that there are essentially
two kinds of people—those who drive trucks, and those
who do not. People who do not drive trucks have to compete with people who drive trucks. And that's not a
pleasant thing, because people who drive trucks have their
own set of rules. I'll go over these in a moment.

But first, you must go buy a truck.

What kind of truck should you buy?

Doesn't matter. Even a little pickup is higher and
longer than most cars. If you are in the hauling business or
cattle business or some business that demands that you
actually pick up something with your pickup, you may
need to consider the size of the bed.

Other than that, you have really only one concern:
What color do you want your truck to be? Look 'em over
and pick one.

EXEMPTIONS

It is possible that you qualify for an exemption from truck ownership. You are not compelled to buy a truck if you:

- Have more than two children. That's because if you have more than two, they won't fit in the cab with you, and hauling them around in the truck bed is a bad idea.

- Have more than two girlfriends. Although putting them all in the truck bed and letting them duke it out might not be such a bad idea.

- Live in one of the big cities and need to parallel park on a regular basis (although if you have a truck you never *have* to park any particular way, as I will explain soon.)

- Are a member of the armed services. What has this got to do with owning a truck? Not a thing. But if you're a member of the armed services and don't want to buy a truck, I'm sure not going to try to twist your arm.

If, for any reason, you are unable to buy a truck, a Suburban or Range Rover or similar high-profile vehicle is an acceptable alternative.

OK. Are you ready to buy that truck? I'll wait while you do that—and while you arrange financing, if necessary, with that cousin who owes you big time.

Got the truck? Fine. Now, perhaps it is you who owe your cousin big time. You must keep these sorts of things in mind, because now that you have a truck, friends and relatives who do not have trucks will be asking you to do any hauling they might need done.

This might include getting their Christmas tree, moving their son to college, or transporting their new refrigerator. Should you do these things? You must make these decisions on a case-by-case basis, but you are never out of line to decline. You can always say you're going to be hauling something else that day. And you are. Ass.

THE RULES

Here are the special rules of the road, just for people who have trucks. A WARNING: These are not the official rules of the Texas Department of Public Safety. They are the unwritten rules that truck-driving Texans live by. Abiding by this set of rules could earn you a traffic ticket—especially in Austin, where the people tend to have an egalitarian attitude, and drivers of cars feel they should have the same rights as drivers of trucks.

But if you are driving a truck and drive it like you'd drive a car, you're going to be considered a wimp.

So here are the rules:

1. Green light means go. Yellow light means go faster. Red light means stop, but it really means it more for cars than for you. You are in a truck. You are going fast, because you have somewhere to be. You are bigger than that stopped car. If the driver of that car has any sense at all, he will not go when the light turns green, because he *knows* that if he does, he will get hit by a truck.

2. Cars must always yield to you. When roads con-
verge, if it's you and a car competing for the same space,
the car must give way—because you're bigger.

3. You do not have to wait in traffic jams. Traffic jams
are a nuisance, almost always involving lots of *cars*. Brown
ones, usually. When traffic forces you to slow to a speed
under 20 miles an hour, you must take evasive action.
First, careen into the lane on the right. Then, cut across
the grass to the nearest frontage road. If this involves
going up or down hills, then yee-ha—it's going to be even
more fun. See, cars can't do this. They have to stay on the
paved roads. Half the fun is watching them glare while
you roll off the road, down the hill, onto the side road,
and off into the distance. (Police officers, of course, take a
very dim view of this practice and have been known to
stage roundups a block from the place where everybody's
cutting across the grass.)

4. Here's an option for getting around traffic jams
when there is no access road you can cut across the grass
to: Simply make the shoulder your own personal lane.
Drive down it until you're past the traffic jam. Wave to any
policemen you see along the way. Wave to the car drivers
who glare at you.

5. Don't bother with your turn signals. You're a truck.
You can go where you want to; why tell anyone ahead of
time?

6. Park wherever you would like to park. You do not
have to have a parking space. You simply need to find an
amount of ground—either paved or unpaved—that is at
least as big as your truck. If you find such a place and are
happy with it, it's your parking space. If you're at a restaurant picking up some food and you can't find a parking

space within 10 feet of the door, feel free to block other diners with your truck. I found myself blocked by a truck once after a meal, but when its driver appeared five minutes later and offered his explanation—"I was just going in to get some food"—I was immediately placated. He was, after all, driving a truck. He had places to be. He was hungry. I was, in fact, in *his* way because my *car* was parked where he would have liked to have parked his truck. But he couldn't, so he had to block me. In the final analysis, it was all my fault for not having a truck. (I am exempt under Section 3 of the exemptions, but that doesn't mean life's going to be easy for me.)

7. If the car in front of you is going too slowly, drive two inches from his bumper. When he checks the rearview mirror, assume a demonic countenance. He'll get out of your way.

8. Anyone wishing to ride beside you in the cab must yell "Shotgun!" when you announce your intention to go somewhere. The first one to so yell gets to sit up front with you. Your other friends, if they want to come along, will need to ride in the truck bed. (That's unless you have one of those extended cabs, in which case you can cram them into the back seat.) The person riding shotgun has the responsibility of opening any gates that you come across along the way to wherever you're going. But unless that's across a pasture, he won't have anything to do but drink beer and relax.

9. You can do anything in your pickup truck that you want to do. The place is virtually a second home. Have dinner in there if you like. Fight with your wife, gesturing wildly and looking at her rather than the road. It's *your* truck. So you make the rules.

TRUCKS AND FRIENDSHIP

Needless to say, the truck comes first.

It is probably a bad idea to let your friends borrow your truck. Invariably, they'll do something to it. Best case scenario: You'll get a cigarette burn on the seat. Worst case: Your truck will be on the nightly news, halfway into somebody's living room.

"Oops," the friend will say. "I'm really sorry. It was an accident. I didn't mean to do that."

That is your cue, as far as the friend is concerned, to say, "That's all right. It would be different if you *meant* to screw up my truck, but since it was an accident, we'll forget all about it. Wanna beer?"

But in truth, your reaction is likely to be more along the lines of "Gosh darnit, C.W., you wrecked my truck!" Your friend, who didn't mean to do it, will not understand this reaction. Y'all won't be sharing beers for quite a while.

So, to save the friendship, keep your truck to yourself.

ACCESSORIZING YOUR TRUCK

The following are accessories that you should consider for your truck:

A dog.

Or, if you are a hunter, multiple dogs. Please refer to the next chapter for information on how to select an appropriate Texas dog. But once you have one, he will expect to ride in the back of your truck. Dogs somehow know how to travel happily in the back of a pickup without falling out. You, however, must do your part in trying not to come to a hasty stop. In that event, your dog could become a dangerous projectile.

There has been much discussion as to what other animals can serve as appropriate truck bed accessories, and the fact is, nothing works as well as a dog. I have seen calves riding in pickup truck beds, but they do not seem particularly happy. Emus, ostriches, hens and such need to be in cages.

Forget cats.

Before taking your dog out on the open road, drive him around awhile near where you live, so that he can get used to seeing other people in cars without barking at them. The dog must feel at home in your truck bed. You might try putting a pillow or towel back there for him to lie on. He can have a favorite toy, but a ball is a bad idea.

Gun rack.

There are several reasons you might wish to have a gun rack in your truck. One is that you have a gun. Hunters frequently use guns and transport them in their trucks.

But you don't have to have a gun in order to have a gun rack. The rack can also house handsaws and other small, elongated implements.

Or perhaps you'd simply like to adopt a menacing demeanor while you're on the road. Having a gun rack in your truck is one way to do so without being overtly aggressive. It might make your fellow drivers think twice before they flip you off for riding their bumpers when they're in the way.

Fuzzy dice.

These hang from the rear view mirror and are merely decorative. Do not attempt to play dice games with them.

Big ol' lights.

These can be mounted on the top of your cab. They can help illuminate dark fields when you're hunting, and they're helpful in locating frogs if you're going frog-gigging. Shine a light on a frog and he will just sit there, motionless, waiting to be gigged. Or perhaps your lights could spot a treed possum, if that's what you're after. But the most common usage seems to be illuminating a nearby beer keg, so that everybody can find it. The most important thing is that these big lights are big and will impress your friends.

Big ol' tires.

Same deal. Impress your friends. You can make your truck even higher than it is anyway by putting huge tires on it. That way, you'll be *way* up in the air and can literally roll over anything that gets in your way.

Toolbox.

Preferably a big one that fits across the width of your pickup bed. Having a toolbox conveys the message that you are a man with tools.

You have places to go and things to fix.

Camper top.

This is optional, but if you have a truck and somehow wind up with more than two children, carpeting the bed and placing a camper top over it is one way to transport them with some small degree of safety. That doesn't make it a station wagon, but it makes your truck into more of a family vehicle—which may or may not be what you're after.

BUMPER STICKERS

These are *very* important. These, along with your driving attitude and proper employment of accessories, will communicate to the world that you are a serious truck guy.

Some popular truck bumper stickers includes:

- "I (heart) my truck."
- "I wasn't born in Texas, but I got here as quick as I could."
- "NRA." (This is the National Rifle Association. You don't have to belong to it to use the bumper sticker. Like the gun rack, it's a deterrent to people getting hostile toward you just because you drive like you think you own the road—which, of course, you do.)
- "Matter of fact, I do own the road."
- "If you can read this, you're too !@#$#@ close!"
- "Back the Blue." This connotes a love for police. It is said to cut down on the number of tickets you receive.

- "Hell yes I'm drunk—What do you think I am? A stunt driver?"
- "Texas is cattle country. So eat beef, you bastards."
- "My kid and my drug money go to the University of Texas."
- "Honk if I'm an Aggie."
- "My kid beats up your honor student."
- "Beautify Texas. Put a Yankee on a bus."
- "Welcome to Texas: Now go home."
- "Cover me. I'm changing lanes."

You get the idea. The more of these you have on your bumper, the more hilarity you will provoke in the truck behind you—assuming the driver can get close enough to read your messages.

OK, NOW WHAT?

Drive, silly.

In the mood for food? Take your truck out for some lunch. A cafeteria is always a good choice, but any restaurant will do as long as it's one frequented by other pickup truck drivers. Look for 'em in the parking lot. A place with a parking lot full of pickup trucks probably serves good food in large portions.

Then, take a spin down to the Home Depot and pick up something. Anything. Grab a furnace filter, a few light bulbs, and several rolls of duct tape—everybody needs duct tape. Throw 'em in the bed of your new pickup with all the new bumper stickers on it. Tool on home.

Put in the furnace filter, screw in the light bulbs (get some help if this poses a problem), and tape up a few things. Then get some beer out of the refrigerator, put it in your truck bed, and haul ass.

Chapter 6

YOUR WIFE AND YOUR DOG

Aside from your truck, these are the most important acquisitions you will make. (Women: For you it's your dog and your husband. We'll get into your perspective later in the chapter.)

Men: Why do you need a wife? Because you have things to do—like haul ass—and you don't need to waste time doing things like overcooking the vegetables, acquiring beers, and cleaning and cooking the quail you bagged. Those jobs belong to your wife. Besides, wives are fun.

The first thing you need to know is how to pronounce the word *wife*.

Remember in Chapter 3, how we discussed elongating those *i*'s until you run out of air? This is a perfect example:

Wiiiiiiiiiiiiiiiiiiiiiiiiiiiiife.

That's how you say it. Try this:

Pretend you're a possum. Somebody has just stepped on your tail. Open your mouth as wide as it will go and bray:

Miiiiii wiiiiiiiiiiiiiiiiiiiife!

There you go. Anytime you start a sentence with "my wife," those two words should take up about 5 seconds.

SELECTING A WIFE

Texas women are a hearty bunch. From the beginning, they've had to be.

The early settlers' wives had to live in a hot, dusty state surrounded by Native Americans—the guys with feathers once known as Indians—who were in a bad mood about having their land swiped. They also had to contend with Native Mexicans, who were in a bad mood about having their land swiped. Most of the Texas men were usually off dealing with cows. The women were left home to tend the kids, wash the clothes, fend off attackers, and sweat. Not much of a life.

Eventually, of course, the Native Americans and Mexicans got used to the swiping and calmed down. Then air conditioning was invented. Things are definitely better now.

But Texas women are still some of the heartiest ol' gals you'll ever want to meet. My point is that the local gene pool is really good, should you be arriving in this state without a wife.

A Texas wife, regardless of category, should be able to handle certain basic tasks, such as baiting her own fish hook and cooking chili. She must be able to deal with heat, hail, and small children without becoming overly nervous. To determine whether she'll work out, you might want to go fishing with her on a hot day when storms are forecast. Invite along a small tribe of noisy children. If she is still speaking to you by the end of the day, it might work out.

Beyond the basics, though, there are several different types of Texas wives:

■ **The trophy wife.** This is the gal with the big hair—and maybe the big bank account, too, if you're lucky. The trophy wife's value is in her looks, her charm, and her ability to entertain on a moment's notice. She knows all the right caterers to call, and her nails never have chips in the enamel. It is important not to confuse a trophy wife with a bimbo, though the two share some characteristics. A bimbo is gorgeous but has never grown, and will never grow, a brain. This situation may be cute at first, but do you really want to be married to somebody who gets the TV remote mixed up with the wireless telephone and can't figure out why there's no dial tone? Bimbos aren't marriage material. Trophy wives aren't (usually) rocket scientists, but they do have basic native intelligence. And what they can't do, they can *hire* done. The trophy wife does carry some risks: (1) She's expensive. She will run up a huge bill at Neiman Marcus, and you can expect to eat out every night. (Cooking would ruin her manicure.) (2) Somebody else might steal her. (3) She may not be the sharpest knife in the drawer. (4) You can't dismiss the possibility that, at some point, she might become a contender in the worst wife contest. (This contest and its rules will be discussed later in this chapter.) But while she's there, she will light up your life with the highlights in her hair.

- **The good ol' gal.** This is a wife who, although she may not be the best-looking ol' gal in the cafeteria, will be good to you and the kids and will never win the worst wife contest. Remember, *ol'* has nothing to do with age; it's a fond expression. A good ol' gal can bait her fish hook with one hand and toss you a beer with the other. And she won't get confused and pour the beer into the fish. Such a woman is to be admired.
- **The sweet little thang.** This is a cute, usually small (but not necessarily) woman whose head you will perpetually have the urge to pat. She's just so cute and sweet. She wears those long, loose dresses and likes to cook, but she's not as tough as a good ol' gal. You may have to clean your own catch. The value of this type of wife is her complete agreeability. She agrees with everything you say. She smiles. She nods. She backs up your fish stories.
- **The fantasy wife.** This is this big Texas man's fantasy: A woman who will make love passionately all night long, then turn into a chicken-fried steak at midnight. This has never happened. But you can dream.

UNDESIRABLE WIVES

There are some women you should run from immediately. You truly should give absolutely no thought to acquiring a wife who:

- Is more nervous than your cat.
- Sheds more than your dog.

- Faxes replies to your love letters.
- Complains about having to climb in and out of your truck.
- Thinks she'll be devoured by skeeters and chiggers if she steps outdoors.
- Puts beans in chili.
- Believes everything she hears on The Weather Channel.

THE WORST WIFE CONTEST

This contest exists in every Texas man's head, and Texas men compare notes every now and then to see if they can agree upon a winner. Every wife in Texas is entered in this contest, though she probably doesn't know it. On starry Texas nights, the tale-telling begins:

"I'll tell you who the winner of the worst wife contest is: It was that Elmyra who was married to ol' Joe down in Nacogdoches, who never would come out of the bathroom except to microwave herself another bag of popcorn."

"Nah, my first wife was the worst wife. She hated my friends, she hated my dogs, she hated *me*. Woulda never kept her around so long, but she made the best chili in Texas."

That sort of thing.

It goes without saying that you don't actually want your wife—not your current one, anyway—to win this contest. And your wife certainly doesn't want to win this contest. It doesn't hurt to let her know it exists. That way, you can win her affection by occasionally whispering into her ear those words she longs to hear: "Darlin', you ain't winnin' the worst wife contest." She'll be so happy.

REBUILDING THE WIFE

As your wife plows steadily through middle age—especially if she is a trophy wife—she may reach the conclusion that her cheeks sag, her breasts are too small, her thighs are too big, her eyelids droop, or she has too many chins. These observations may be accurate or simply the result of too much mirror-gazing. But when a Texas wife becomes convinced that she needs an overhaul, nothing will do but to call in the plastic surgeon.

Texas women keep scores of facelift doctors busy in every major city. Some like the procedure so well that they get lifted and lifted and lifted until their eyes are pretty much at scalp level and you can bounce a quarter off their cheeks. At this point, face lifting has become recreational.

For the most part, though, a little dab'll do it. She'll get her nose bobbed into a cute little ski jump and get that chin tucked back where it was. Tell her she looks perfect. Then there's an outside chance she won't want to have a little more carving done next year—except maybe at Thanksgiving.

A WORD ABOUT SECRETARIES

It is a well-known fact to every Texas wife that fat women over the age of 50 make the best secretaries. So yours had better be. Maybe the best course is just to hire an "assistant."

WIFEZE

Most Texas wife language is the same as wife language the world over. "I don't want to talk about it," means "I want to talk about it," and "Whatever you want, dear," means "All right, but you're going to pay for this, one way or the other."

But there's one phrase you need to watch out for with Texas women.

If you hear your wife talking about another woman and using the words "bless her heart," you can be sure that the wife's claws are out and some major disparagement in under way. To wit:

"Mary just can't seem to lose those extra 15 pounds she picked up in the South of France, bless her heart."

The proper response to any heart-blessing is a simple grunt or shake of the head. You must not acknowledge that you know the wife is being tacky. It ruins the whole effect of the heart-blessing.

SELECTING A HUSBAND

This is not as intricate a process as wife selection, because there are fewer species of Texas men.

The bad news: There's no such thing as a trophy husband. Sorry. There *are* male equivalents of bimbos. I call them bimbobs. They're beautiful but brainless. Not marriage material.

Here are a few types of Texas men to choose from:

- **The good ol' boy.** Most plentiful species. Enjoy their lives, enjoy their wives, enjoy just sitting in front of the TV flipping channels. Love getting together with other good ol' boys. These have faults. They may snore, sweat, and leave the toilet seat up. Some of them have no visible means of support. But they're basically good ol' boys, and that's why you love 'em.

- **The good OLD boy.** This one has lived long enough to accumulate vast sums of money. Assuming he has a decent personality, he's husband material. There's a saying among Texas women: It's as easy to love a rich man as a poor one. (The guys, of course, are hearing the same thing about women from their dads.)

- **The cowboy.** He's cute. He's polite to a fault, he smiles all the time, and he cleans up good. So what's the downside? *You'll never know his feelings.* He'll keep you wondering till the day he dies.

The good OLD boy. This one has lived long enough to accumulate vast sums of money. Assuming he has a decent personality, he's husband material.

INAPPROPRIATE HUSBANDS

- **The plastic explosive.** Gosh, he seemed like a nice guy. He was everything you ever wanted in every way. After kissing your share of frogs, you married this Prince Charming and—ka-BAM!—he blew up, and in his place is an unemployed goon. This is not the husband you ordered. The trick is to peel off the paint and expose the goon before you marry him.
- **Mister Me.** He'll talk for hours about himself, then ask how *you* feel about him. If there's a tornado in Missouri, he'll try to figure out what the impact is on him. He has trouble buying a cowboy hat because there's not one big enough to fit his swollen head. There's no room for you in this guy's life. It's full, thank you.

YOUR DAWG

Despite the fact that you may have a wife or husband, you also need a dawg. Your dawg serves many purposes:
- He is your best friend. He is loyal and will follow you around the house, quietly sitting at your feet, demanding nothing. He never wants to discuss his feelings.
- He helps you hunt for things. He can help you hunt for deer or quail, or he might just help you hunt for your keys. Not that he knows where your keys are. But if

you ask him enthusiastically to find them, he'll bound off happily, thereby raising your spirits to the point where you have a better chance of finding your keys.

- He barks and growls where appropriate.
- He can slay bugs. Dogs love chasing bugs. My husband once had a dog named Puddy Lou who was a great roacher. She would catch a cockroach and carry it carefully—her teeth just barely clutching the edge of the roach. (She didn't like the taste of roach.) She would lay the night's catch out at my husband's feet for approval. Too bad she never learned to flush them down the commode.
- He laughs at your jokes. Fact is, he looks like he's laughing all the time. For he's a jolly good fellow.

CHOOSING A DAWG

As a Texan, you need a serious dawg. If you already have a silly little fluffy dog that yaps, you may keep it. But you will need to add at least one real dawg—a fairly large one that really *barks* and is big enough to warm your feet when he lays on the end of the bed.

Here are some possibilities:

Hound dawg. A truly great dawg. He hunts, he wags his tail, he's loyal, and he prefers that you leave the toilet seat up in case he gets really thirsty.

Pit bull. He has that "Don't Mess with Me" look on his face, and he walks the right walk. Trouble is, he's had a lot of bad press for biting people. So make sure he doesn't do that.

Beagle. Keeps his nose to the ground doing whatever it is you want him to do, whether it's hunting or just walkin' around. Good in the back of a pickup. His bark is definitely bigger than his bite. This is the loudest of all possible curs. A Texas dawg, to be sure.

Golden Retriever. You may have nothing for him to retrieve, but he doesn't mind. He's just glad to be in the same world with you.

Labrador Retriever. Ditto.

Basset hound. Has friends in low places.

Bulldog. It's the look on the face. Very Texas.

Doberman. The little cut-off ears are silly, but he's a tough dog, so you've got to respect him.

Great Dane. If you want to run with the big dawgs, this is the guy for you. These animals are huge. There is nothing you can name that is anything like a Dane. Warning: They like to lean on people they like.

Mutt. Probably your best bet. A dawg of mixed heritage has a varied perspective on life, which means he doesn't have any idea what's going on, and he doesn't care. He's a dawg, is all. Great attitude.

UNSUITABLE DAWGS

Li'l ol' yappy dawgs. They're yappy and they're little. What more is there to say?

Dawgs that'll bite you. Actually, I once knew of a dog whose name was Did He Bite You? But it was all run together and came out Diddeebatcha. Diddeebatcha was a yappy little dawg, too. Bad news all the way around. Most dawgs know not to bite the hand that feeds 'em. If your dawg hasn't figured this out, he's the wrong dawg to have.

Dawgs that like mailmen. There are only a few reasons why your dawg might like the mailman, and all of them are bad. Don't trust a dawg who doesn't try to devour anybody in a uniform carrying letters. And if he likes the mailman better than you, you should probably get rid of the dawg *and* the wife.

Corny dogs. These are the best food at the State Fair of Texas, but they cannot be domesticated. Just eat 'em.

NAMING YOUR DAWG

In a state where there are men named Buster and Blackie and Boo, it probably should be stated for the record that your dawg should not have the same name as you. It would confuse the neighbors when your wife went out on the porch and yelled.

Texas dawgs have been named just about everything. But most Texas dawgs have good, strong names to match the strength of their owners.

I know a bulldog named Tank. He's huge, he's strong, he's a dawg's dawg. In reality, of course, he's sweet and docile. But nobody seeing that dawg swagger down the street will know that.

Other good Texas dog names: Blue, Buster (unless it's your name, of course), Bruiser, Killer, Sam (it just sounds good on a dog), and Impervious.

If your dog is a breed and you want to register him with the American Kennel Club, go ahead. But realize that you will have to also come up with a name you can also *call* the dog. AKC names have to be long and weird, because, like actors, each dog must have a name completely different from all the others. So you wind up naming your dog Most Obsequious Theodore of Euless. You don't want your wife shouting that from the front porch. So you nickname him Growler.

THE HIGHLAND PARK EXCEPTION

OK, there is one place where you can have a little, yappy, fluffy, ridiculous dog, and that is in Highland Park, that little enclave within Dallas where dogs are all blow-dried, and nobody's allowed to truly bark.

A Highland Park bumper sticker reads: "I brake for show dogs." They mean it, too.

Chapter 7

EATIN' AND DRANKIN'

These are the two most important activities for a Texan, with the possible exception of drivin' your truck—and, actually, you can eat and drank while drivin' your truck. So dig in and rare back.

Eatin' and drankin' go hand in hand, so this chapter is designed to tell you what food to have in one hand and what drank to have in the other.

Drank, of course, is both a noun and a verb. Outside of Texas, the word is "drink." But in Texas, it is "drank."

Confused? Worried about verb tenses? Here's how it goes:

Present tense: Drank.

Past tense: Drank.

What you become after you drank: Drunk.

"Eat," you will be relieved to know, is the same in Texan as it is in other North American languages.

That having been established, we move on to the six basic food groups of Texas:

- Chili
- Barbecue
- Fried stuff
- Mushy vegetables
- Mexican food
- Beer

It is recommended that each week you consume at least two servings each from the chili group and Mexican food group, three each from the barbecue group and fried stuff group, and six from the mushy vegetable group, along with at least ten servings from the beer group.

Let's take them one at a time and explore the wonders of Texas cuisine: (Vegetarians, please skip to the section on Mushy Vegetables; the rest of this stuff will gross you out.)

CHILI

Chili is the official state dish of Texas. It was so proclaimed in 1977. And if you know beans about chili, you know that Texas chili has no beans. Under no circumstances are beans to be introduced into this dish. I cannot stress this strongly enough.

If you put beans in your chili, you will be immediately identified as someone Not From Around Here, and you will be invited to go back There.

Chili is taken very seriously in Texas. Some years back, the venerable annual chili cookoff in Terlingua became so combative that it divided into two competing chili cook-offs. But despite their differences, all the chili-heads agree on one thing: There are no beans in chili.

There has been a disturbing trend in recent years to infest chili with corn. This *chili con corn* is a con and must be stricken from your recipe book.

The basis of chili is meat—usually some sort of steak or, for informal chili, ground beef. Ground turkey is OK, if you're into losing weight or saving cows. Chili has been made from deer, goat, ostrich, snake, and armadillo and . . . well, you don't want to know what else.

But not beans.

I trust I have made my point.

Competition chili is served to judges in white foam cups, without any garnish whatsoever. (You garnish it and you're out of the contest.)

But when you make chili at home and serve it to your family, you are allowed to add chopped onions and/or grated cheese.

But *no beans.*

It is only right that I give you, at this point, a recipe for chili.

Recipe For Chili: Go to the grocery store. Buy a pound of lean ground beef, an 8-oz. can of tomato sauce and a Wick Fowler's brand chili kit. Follow the directions. The result will be bona fide Texas chili, as good as any-body else's.

Also in the Chili Group you will find:

- Chili-rice. As the saying goes, chili-rice is very nice. This is prepared by serving the chili in a bowl over rice. Top it with cheese and onions.
- Frito Pie. Get a small bag of Fritos. (They are a Texas product and should be consumed with pride.) Open the bag. Pour in chili. Add cheese and onions if you like. Grab a spoon and dig in.

Chili is a hot food and should always be consumed with a cold longneck beer to quench the fiery furnace that your stomach has become. A Tums chaser wouldn't hurt.

Common mistakes made with chili:

- Adding too much tomato sauce. If tomato is the overriding taste, you've got spaghetti sauce, not chili. The bit of tomato sauce in chili is there to make it a bit reddish, but it shouldn't look like a melted down fire truck.
- Infesting the chili with *beans.* (You will be caught. Stop now, before it's too late.)
- Spelling it *chile.* Chile is a country. Chile is a pepper. The stuff in the bowl is *chili.*

For further reading on chili, I refer you to the seminal work *A Bowl of Red,* by the late great chili-head Frank Tolbert.

BARBECUE

What makes Texas barbecue wonderful is *smoke.* The smoky taste provides that indescribably wonderful feeling that grips your body when your mouth communes with a late cow or pig.

Forget about what you have come to know as barbecue: charcoal-cooked baby back ribs, pulled pork, or that Sloppy Joe stuff.

Texas barbecue is slow-smoked in a big pit. Barbecue is most often brisket. Also popular are big ol' beef ribs, pork ribs, and sausage. (Elgin, Texas—pronounced El-gan with a hard "g,"—is famous for its sausage, known as "hot-guts.")

Meat is slow-smoked on a pit stoked with wood to which mesquite is generally added. When the meat is sliced, there is a defined pink area—called a smoke ring —on the outer edge. The better defined the smoke ring, the finer the barbecue is considered to be.

In many popular Texas barbecue spots, you're served a big mess of the stuff not on a plate, but on a piece of butcher paper. No sauce.

The only garnish might be a slice of onion, pickle, and some saltines surrounding a tall pyramid of meat, smoky and wonderful.

The smoking pits inside these places are often so huge that customers, too, become smoked. Your hair will smell like barbecue until you wash it, and in the unhappy event that you were to be sliced, you would doubtless have a nice pink smoke ring.

There are some barbecue chains—Dallas-based Sonny Bryan's for one—that have sauce, and it's great sauce. The place is too popular with tourists not to have sauce. But the smoke's the important part.

The type of sauce served in barbecue establishments varies depending on which part of the state you're in. In

East Texas, for example, the sauce tends to be thick and rather sweet. In Central Texas, the sauce will be thin and probably based on meat drippings.

Also in the barbecue group:

- Barbecued chicken
- Goat, called *cabrito*. It's tougher than cow, but a lot of Texans swear by it. It's often on the menus of Mexican restaurants.
- Meats and fish cooked on your backyard grill with charcoal, as long as you remember to throw in a few mesquite chips.

FRIED STUFF

All good Texans love the lard. And there is no sound more thrilling to the ears of a Texan than the sizzling of fat in the kitchen.

There is one fried dish that, above all, epitomizes Texas culinary achievement: the chicken-fried steak.

If you haven't had one of these, stop reading, get into your car, drive immediately to the nearest restaurant, and order one.

The chicken-fried steak: a plate-sized, pounded, inexpensive cut of steak, very heavily battered and fried until it is crispy, then smothered in white gravy. (There might even be an air pocket in there. Does it go "whoosh" when you dig in?) This thing will make your arteries stand up and salute. It's ubiquitous on Texas menus. I even saw it featured as the daily special once in a Dallas Chinese restaurant.

Do not agonize over whether to serve chicken-fried steak with red wine (because it's a steak) or white (because it's *chicken*-fried). The answer is neither: Chicken-fried steak should be consumed with beer.

Also in the fried stuff group:

- Chicken-fried chicken. This may seem redundant, but it's not. Regular fried chicken is floured, then fried in a skillet. Chicken-fried chicken is heavily battered and fried *as though* it were a chicken-fried steak. Hence, chicken-fried chicken.

- Fried catfish. Use cornmeal. Don't try to chicken-fry a catfish.

- Hush puppies. Fried rounds of cornmeal.

- Calf fries. Perhaps you have already tried these succulent little oyster-like morsels and wondered what they were. There's no easy way to say this: They're testicles. Well, there are a lot of steers in Texas. What were they supposed to do with all those byproducts? Fry 'em. Always a good answer.

- Fried pies. These are those little folded-over pies that are deep-fried. You can buy them mass-produced at the store, but if you're really brave you can make them at home. Make your regular pie crust, place some apple pie filling inside, then drop it in and watch it absorb all that wonderful fat. Grease is the word.

- Corn dogs. Invented nearly 50 years ago at the Texas State Fair, Fletcher's original hot dog on a stick, surrounded by thick cornmeal breading, is an institution. As a Texan, you must slather it with yellow mustard before consuming it. And no, the ones you buy in the grocery store will never taste the same.

- Fried okra. Although okra is generally considered a staple of the Mushy Vegetables group, it crosses over when it is fried. Cornmeal is the breading of choice. Fried okra is a highly acceptable choice for those of us Texans who are reluctant to be slimed by the boiled version.

- Corn bread. It's in this category because you make it in a frying pan—a big cast-iron skillet. That officially makes it fried.

To make fried stuff: Get a big vat of grease and throw in the stuff. Fry it till it's light brown and has soaked up a good bit of grease. And if at first you don't succeed, fry, fry again.

MUSHY VEGETABLES

Texas mamas taught their babies to overcook vegetables, but you'll have to learn the hard way.

If there's one thing a Texan cannot stand, it's an *al dente* green bean. Boil those suckers till they keel over.

Texans' love for mushy vegetables laced with hog fat or bacon grease is doubtless the reason for the incredible popularity of cafeterias. Go walk out in your front yard, look in all directions, and name the cafeterias within five miles of your house. Got at least five of 'em, right? The Texas landscape is riddled with cafeterias. And they all serve mushy vegetables.

You should eat at a cafeteria at least twice a week. If you attend church, one of those times can be on Sunday after church. If you do not attend church, avoid going to the cafeteria on Sundays. You will have to compete with the churchgoers for your favorite mushy vegetables, and they will glower at you for wearing shorts to the cafeteria on Sunday.

The best-loved Texas vegetable is the black-eyed pea. When served in a cold salad with jalapenos, black-eyed peas are called Texas caviar and treated with commensurate respect. When you hear the word "pea" in Texas, do not think of those green things. If you wish to discuss those, you must say "English peas." A "pea" in Texas, unless otherwise modified, is presumed to be a black-eyed pea.

These are little brown peas with black spots (eyes, if you will). You will eat them on New Year's Day for good luck. You have to. If you don't eat black-eyed peas on New Year's Day, everyone will be afraid to go near you.

If you don't like them now, don't worry. They'll grow on you. Before you know it, you'll be ready for the black-eyed pea's cousins, purple hulls, cream peas, and field or "cow" peas.

How to cook black-eyed peas: Put four or five cups of water in a big pot. Toss in a small piece of salt pork, hog jowl, or slice of bacon. Boil vigorously for 10 minutes. Lower heat to low and pour in a pint of fresh-shelled black-eyed peas. (You can find them at a roadside stand, farmer's market, or a few big-on-produce grocery stores.) Simmer with lid on for 35 minutes. Within the last 10 minutes, add 4 to 6 drops of Tabasco, 4 to 6 drops of pepper sauce, salt and pepper to taste, and just a dash of sugar (but never admit you put sugar in your peas). Don't overcook the peas or they'll be tough.

It would not be a bad idea to cook some black-eyed peas while you continue reading this book. Take a break and go buy some, now.

Got the peas? Are they on the stove? OK. Here are some other foods in the Mushy Vegetable group:

■ Okra. The slimiest of vegetables, it has found great favor here, especially among male Texans. No matter how they are cooked, they will be mushy on the inside. However, if the Mushy Vegetable group is not your favorite, you may fry your okra.

■ Smashed taters. They are not mashed. They are not whipped. They are smashed.

■ Cream style corn. On the cob it's not mushy enough.

■ Greens. Any kind: collards, turnip greens, mustard green, whatever—cooked in large quantities of animal fat. Otherwise, they'd be too healthy and you'd be in California.

■ Macaroni and cheese. I know, I know: There is nothing mildly vegetative about either macaroni or cheese. But take a look at the menu at your favorite home-cooking Texas restaurant, under vegetables. Chances are, you'll find macaroni and cheese listed. And every cafeteria offers macaroni and cheese as a vegetable. Texas children love macaroni and cheese, especially if it comes from a box.

MEXICAN FOOD

Mexican food is well known throughout Texas for its curative powers. It can mend a broken heart, cool a serious mad, and—best of all—dispose of a hangover better than any other type of food.

By Mexican food, I generally mean Tex-Mex, the great confluence of cultures. There are some authentic Mexican restaurants in Texas that offer cuisine from the interior of

Mexico. But for the most part, we're talkin' enchiladas and tacos and such.

Mexican food always comes on a very hot plate. You'll know your favorite Mexican joint has decided you are a real Texan when the waiters stop yelling "Hot plate!" when they throw your food in front of you.

A key ingredient of Mexican food is the jalapeno.

These little ol' green peppers will show up on just about everything you eat, so you would do well to acquire a taste for them. Bring along Tums or Rolaids until your digestive tract has built up the requisite armor-plating.

Nachos are ubiquitous in Texas, and in Mexican restaurants, heavy with ingredients and slathered with Mexican *queso*, they're terrific. Real *nachos* bear no resemblance to the dead chips with orange goo that you get at baseball parks—although chips-and-goo are top sellers at Texas ballparks. Better a bad *nacho* than no *nacho* at all.

Menudo is Mexican tripe stew. It's supposed to be one of the very best hangover cures, but only an *hombre muy macho* will eat the stuff. It'll put lead in your pencil.

Salsa is slathered over everything in Texas. You're probably familiar with the stuff, because in recent years it has overtaken ketchup as the most popular condiment in the country. Now that you're a Texan, you must pour more—and hotter—*salsa* over everything you eat. Everything; not just Mexican food. It's really great on mushy vegetables.

The proper accompaniment to a Mexican meal is a margarita or a Mexican beer. Among the best beers: Dos Equis, Bohemia, Carta Blanca, Superior, and Tecate. And OK, if you're a college student, Corona with a lime is acceptable.

Making Mexican food at home: Are you Mexican? If so, you know how. If you're not Mexican, why would you want to attempt this? Mexican restaurants are good, plentiful, and cheap. And their plates are hotter than yours.

ONIONS

And now, a word about onions, which aren't mushy and thus can't be included in the Mushy Vegetable group. They're sometimes fried—but not often enough to be included in the Fried Stuff group. So they're just sort of there. But they must be discussed, because Texas onions are wonderful.

If you are from Georgia, you are going to have to drop all allegiance to Vidalia onions in favor of Texas 1015s. I know; it's a silly name for an onion. But the Texas A&M scientist who came up with these onions apparently used up all his creativity coming up with the onion and didn't have any left to think up a name.

Aggie scientists are always inventing new vegetables, and some of them are silly. They once invented a non-hot jalapeno—a not-so-hot idea if ever there was one. But the guy who invented 1015s was having a very, very good day. These are exquisite onions—sweet and crunchy. They're often served just sitting there by themselves instead of on things. You will love them.

An East Texas specialty is the Noonday onion, so called because it's grown in Noonday, Texas. Also very sweet.

BEER

Nobody has ever figured out how a longneck bottle improves the taste of Lone Star beer, but it does. The long neck also provides a nice handle for retrieval from an ice chest—an act that gives a Texas beer-drinker satisfaction similar to that experienced during the extraction of a nice bass from a lake.

Texas-brewed Shiner is also an excellent beer. Also popular: the ubiquitous Miller Lite, Coors, and Bud. When possible, buy longnecks—unless you have to carry the cooler a long way, in which case cans are fine.

Real Texans do not consume wine coolers.

If you are a non-imbiber, the Texas beverage of choice is iced tea. It is mandatory to have iced tea with cafeteria food. And on all occasions when you are not in a beer-related frame of mind, iced tea is appropriate. It's served in a tall tumbler with lots of ice, and restaurants will give you a second glass free.

If you are in a drankin' mood and prefer a cocktail to beer, the margarita is the state favorite. Beware of Texas cocktails that have jalapenos floating in them. Only hard-core jalapenists should consume these. One restaurant in South Padre Island offers a jalapeno martini as its constant special. It's cheap, and that makes it tempting—but be advised they will not serve the jalapeno on the side. If you want the martini cheap, it must be infested with a jalapeno, and even if you remove the jalapeno, an oil slick will remain. The bottom line: You don't have to quaff jalapenos to be a real Texan. Why not just eat them and stick to drankin' beeer?

Back to beer: You should be aware that it does have a few unpleasant side effects if consumed in excess quantities. A few examples:

- You forget the proper conjugation of the verb *to drank*.
- The floor turns sideways, and you fall off.
- You have an argument with the shrubbery, and the shrubbery wins.
- You have an irresistible urge to call someone on the phone and tell him or her exactly what you think. (A

support group has been formed to deal specifically with this problem. It is called SADD—Sisters Against Drunk Dialing. Check the phone book and see if there's one in your town.)

If you suffer from any of these side effects, you should put down your longneck and find the nearest bed or couch. (Forget about going anywhere near your vehicle.) Pass out. When you wake up in the morning, go eat some Mexican food. Pray that it stays down.

Chapter 8

GETTIN' MAD AND GETTIN' EVEN

In Texas, when you get mad you must get even. Period.

HOW YOU KNOW WHEN A TEXAN IS MAD

You've heard that song, "The Eyes of Texas Are Upon You"? Well, if a Texan's eyes are fixed directly upon you and his mouth is a thin straight line and he's a little red in the face—you've done or said something to make him mad, and it's probably time to apologize profusely.

WHEN YOU GET MAD

You have a right to get mad—and, therefore, to get even—when any of the following things occur:

- Somebody touches you. At all. *Especially* if he jabs at you with his finger while making a point.
- Somebody touches your girl. Or even looks at her funny.
- Somebody utters fightin' words.

FIGHTIN' WORDS

You know you're in trouble in Texas if you hear: "Em's fightin' words!" So before you utter any, you'd better know what they are. Fightin' words are something that strike a sour chord in the heart of a Texan by challenging his or her judgment, loyalty, or basic beliefs. Some examples:

"Your wife is ugly."

"Your dog is ugly."

"Your truck is ugly."

"The Alamo is ugly."

"Em's beans in your chili."

To an alumnus of Texas A&M, any laudatory mention of the University of Texas constitutes fightin' words, as does any reference to the changing of light bulbs in the same sentence with "Aggie."

THE STAGES OF GETTING EVEN

Now it's time to get even. Don't ever tell an angry Texan to talk it out. He's likely to let his fingers do the talking—to your eyeballs. OK, the three stages of getting even:

- Offering an insult
- Offering a threat

- Opening a can of Whup-Ass

Occasionally, the first of these is enough to make your opponent back off. If not, then you must proceed to the second.

THE ART OF THE INSULT

When a Texan insults you, you know you've been insulted.

At the 1988 Democratic National Convention, former Texas governor Ann Richards had a doozy for Republican presidential candidate George Bush:

"Poor George," said Ms. Richards with a big Texas smile upon her face. "He was born with a silver foot in his mouth."

Great line. Bush won the election anyway, but it was still a great line.

Here are a few Texas insults that you may apply any time you deem appropriate:

- You're a few tacos shy of a No. 2 dinner.
- Not the sharpest knife in the drawer, are ya?
- You're so dumb, I bet your mama has to water you.
- When you haul ass, you have to make two trips.
- You're a little off plumb, huh?
- Bet your ass has its own congressman.
- You're so ugly, your parents had to tie a pork chop around your neck to get your dog to play with you.
- Your blender doesn't go all the way to puree.

THE RIGHT THREATS

If you have thoroughly insulted your tormentor and he is still there, it is time to threaten him. With a menacing glare, try one of the following:

- I'm gon' kick yer ass.
- I'm gon' bust yer head.
- I'm gon' open up a can of Whup-Ass.

All of these essentially mean the same thing, but depending on what part of his anatomy your antagonist values most, one may be more effective than the others. All, however, boil down to the dreaded opening of the can of Whup-Ass.

CANS OF WHUP-ASS

These can be opened at the drop of a hat, and as I said in Chapter 1, unless you are the one with the can opener, you will not enjoy the contents.

Opening a can of Whup-Ass is, of course, just an expression—although some guy did once market cans of Whup-Ass. My husband wound up with one. He placed it on a shelf in his office. It's been there for about a dozen years, and he says he's never been tempted to open it. He's a quiet man who keeps to himself. But I wouldn't test the man.

So, OK, back to the matter at hand: Under what circumstances should you open a can of Whup-Ass on somebody?

You have the right to reach for the can opener (or flip the pop-top if it's one of those modern cans) when:

- You have wounded your opponent with a creative insult, and he's still standing there staring at you.
- He looks at you the wrong way.
- He will not quit poking you in the chest.
- He goes anywhere near your wife's chest.
- He drinks your beer.
- He is clearly planning to go for the can opener first.

HOW TO OPEN THE CAN OF WHUP-ASS

Carefully, lest the contents spill all over you, too. Remember: Sometimes little guys can trash the tar out of big guys. Feisty little Billy Martin, the late Texas Rangers manager, won a lot of bar fights—usually by landing the first punch. Often a sucker punch. It's really only a fair fight if you win.

DON'T GO OVERBOARD

Texas law is generally fair to Texas adults. But if you fight the law, the law will win. Making holes in people, whether it's with a gun, knife, or whatever, is a bad idea. (A cutting glance is acceptable.) Texas may have a reputation for lawlessness, but the fact is that more people are executed here than anywhere else.

You should familiarize yourself with the following law enforcement types in Texas:

■ **Local Police:** It's pronounced *po*-lice, with the accent on the "po." These are very busy in the big cities, but in the suburbs and many rural areas they don't have a whole lot to do. So they will notice if you go, say, two miles over the speed limit. They will pull you over and give you a ticket. Don't give them any argument or they will also give you a ticket for not signaling when they pulled you over. Be very, very respectful. The words "yes, sir" and "I'm sorry, sir" will go a long way. They might just let you off without a ticket. Avoid such snappy retorts as "Whatsa matter? Hadn't got your quota this month?" or "Was I the only one drivin' slow enough for you to catch?" *This is no time to practice the art of the creative insult.* Go home and get mad there. And don't even *think* about opening a can of Whup-Ass.

- **The sheriff's department.** You will learn that, in all probability, your local sheriff's office still has a posse. This will conjure up images of guys on horse-back rounding up horse thieves in a John Wayne movie. But the chief function of a posse these days is to ride their horses in parades. The sheriff's guys you have to watch out for are the ones in cars. When they're in their cars, they're looking for someone who has broken the law.

- **The Department of Public Safety.** These are the highway patrol guys, and when you're on those long stretches of lonesome highway between, say, Dallas and South Padre Island, they will be watching you. If you exceed the speed limit, they will often write you a ticket. But *in general* they are less strict than the local police. Exceeding the speed limit by two miles in a 70 zone will rarely earn you a ticket. Still, if you get stopped, the right thing to do is apologize profusely and throw in a lot of *sirs*. Hope for deferred adjudication (which essentially means you still have to pay the ticket, but you keep the offense off your record), but be prepared to have to take a defensive driving course to keep your record clean. (Hint: The regular course is funnier than the comedy course.) Again, forget about getting mad or even.

- **The Texas Rangers.** If you are a real badass, the Texas Rangers will come after you. There's no law-enforcement agency like the Texas Rangers anywhere in the world. Before you envision tobacco-chewing marauders flailing at you with baseball bats, I should explain that these Texas Rangers are not the ones who play baseball. These are ones with guns. They become angry only if you do something really out of line, like murdering or trying to form your own country. They are fearless dudes, these "one Ranger, one riot" guys, and they will not hesitate to open a can of Whup-Ass on you without so much as a preliminary verbal skirmish. You've been warned.

Chapter 9

TEXAS BIG HAIR

Instead of covering human beings with fur like he did with most mammals, God decided to put a bunch of hair on our heads and see what we'd do about it. He knew the combination of free will and human vanity would produce some interesting results. And it has—especially in Texas.

Texas hair (say HAY-er) must, like everything else in Texas, be big.

Look at it this way: The taller the hair, the closer to God. Then, too, you can add several inches to your height by enlarging your hair. The person sitting behind you in the movies might not be too happy. But if he says anything, threaten to add a hat.

Hairdressers tell me they follow a process with Texas women: They take whatever hairstyle is current, and they inflate it. If, for example, everybody in the world is getting a bob, Texas women are happy with a *high* bob. If layering is in, just add a little pouf and it'll work in Texas.

Quintessential Texas hair is, of course, big and *blonde*. Doesn't matter what you were born with. You can be a blonde. May as well; everybody else is.

Every now and then, the hairdressers try to take control of this situation and declare, unilaterally, that short brown hair is a good thing. They try to talk their clients into it. But it's kind of like the apparel industry declaring from time to time that mid-calf-length dresses are pretty.

Nobody's buying it. Texas women want their hair big and blonde.

The chief trendsetters in this area are, of course, the Dallas Cowboy Cheerleaders. There they are—dancing, prancing, tossing those huge, curly manes of the world's largest hair, most of it blonde.

From time to time the cheerleaders will hire a hairdresser who feels they need to "update" their look. Press releases will be issued stating that the cheerleaders' hair will be sleeker and more muted in color that particular year.

Never happens.

If the women of Texas can't depend on the Dallas Cowboy Cheerleaders to set an example when it comes to humongous hair, what is the world coming to?

Big hair. That's the ticket. If you don't have it, get it.

GETTING IT

Don't panic if your hair is not naturally big. There are several ways to big it up:

- Perm it. This process makes your head a mass of springy, tight little coils. By tossing your head forward and running your fingers through these coils, you can create truly mammoth hair.

- Curl it yourself. Go to the store and buy a bunch of those little foam rollers. Roll your hair tightly. You should come close to creating the masses of curls that a perm creates—though you may have to curl and re-curl your hair to maintain its enormity. (Hot rollers and curling irons are as important to a Texas woman's home as is a toaster.)

- Tease it. Call it names, if necessary. And if that doesn't work, slap it around a little.

- Rat it. Back-comb the heck out of it, especially at the crown. Ratting—and if you're not sure how to do it, just ask your next-door neighbor—can easily turn a flathead into a twelve-story building.

- Put volumizing goo in it. Ah, that word: *volumize.* When the trend toward verbacizing came into vogue in the '80s, one of the first nouns to be verbed was *volume.* The phrase *to create volume* was deemed too voluminous for the average vocabulary, so the word was born: *volumize.* There are volumizing shampoos, volumizing conditioners, volumizing lotions, and volu-mizing goos of various types. If you use all of these, your limp hair should finally surrender and throw up its hands—and thus look bigger than when it had its hands down to its sides. At that point, your volumiza-tion is complete.

THE BIG BANG THEORY

A word about Texas bangs. If you're going to have them, they can't just sit there sticking to your forehead. They have to look like a tsunami.

These mega-bangs are created by lifting, ratting, and applying curling irons to the point where the bangs are vertical, with only a slight curl toward the forehead. It's a simple exercise, really: Lift and spray, lift and spray. It's all in the wrist. Observe Texas teenage girls. They have it down.

LET US SPRAY

I trust that by now you have employed one of the aforementioned methods, and your hair is large.

Now you have to keep it that way.

Go buy the biggest can of hairspray you can find. Get the volumizing kind. And "extra firm hold." I said a big can. That's why they have all these super-sized Wal-Mart type things in Texas; so that they can sell huge vats of hair spray.

Got the spray? Spray your hair. Spray it again. Spray it again—especially those big bangs.

Do you live in Houston or anywhere to the south of that city? Then spray it five or six times more. Humidity has an amazing ability to de-volumize hair. Spray, spray, spray.

THE FRIZZ FACTOR

There is one exception to the aforementioned decree about humidity. Your hair will not flatten in the humidity if you are blessed with frizzy hair.

If you have frizzy hair, you have the battle of the bigness won. You were born with bigness, and Texas humidity is only going to big it further. Your only challenge is to wrestle the resulting Brillo into some sort of shape. It is generally a losing battle. But I'll get to some possibilities in a minute.

THE BLONDE THING

It is possible that you are not a blonde. You have never been a blonde. You have no intention of becoming a blonde.

Wanna bet?

There's something about moving to Texas that gives a woman the sudden urge to dive headfirst into a bottle of peroxide. Maybe it's something in the air; maybe it's something in the hot sauce.

But hoards of women gallop to their hairdressers daily with the instruction: "Make me blonde!"

They mean really blonde, too. Yellow or lighter. None of these silly muted gold tones.

Are you already a blonde? Then you need highlights. They'll make you even blonder.

The problem this creates is obvious: You must visit your hairdresser about once a month—more frequently if you natural color is far from blonde—to keep from showing (shudder) roots! The problem is exacerbated if you are short. Everybody can see the top of your head.

Texas hairdressers make a mint on hair colorings.

A woman enters a salon.

"This," she will say, pointing to a hank of hair on the hair color chart, "is my natural color."

The hairdresser will shake his head.

"This," he will say, pointing to a shock of gray hair, "is your natural color."

"Oh," she will say, "I mean the color my hair was when I was four."

"You are not four," the hairdresser will reveal. "You are 84. Perhaps Amazingly Bright Yellow would look less than natural on you."

Nevertheless, it's what she wants, and if there's one thing Texas hairdressers have learned, it's that Texas woman are bulldog-tenacious and bulldog-vicious when it comes to their hair.

So when the day comes that you want to become a blonde—or blonder—just find the color you want in a magazine, thrust it under your hairdresser's nose, and yell "Do this!" He will sigh and do it.

YO, MEN

Did you think I had forgotten you?

You can't just sit there watching your wife's big hair. You have an obligation to do the best by your own hair, too.

If at all possible, make it big. Probably the best way is to adopt Televangelist Hair. Have your hairdresser cut your hair long on top, short on the sides. The blow dry should be up and back—lift and curl. A big round brush will help. And, OK, rat it—but don't tell anybody. Nothing's worse than having a friend rat on your ratting.

Get that nice lift established, then spray, spray, spray.

Then go drink a beer so Bubba and the boys don't catch the smell of hairspray on you.

123

HAT HAIR

This is a problem for both sexes in Texas because of the popularity of cowboy hats.

If you've been wearing a hat for several hours and then remove it, you're going to have a halo-like ridge around your hair. You can comb, you can brush, you can spray: That ridge is there to stay until you wash your hair again. It's sort of like when you walk into a barbecue joint and your hair smells like a brisket till you wash it. Hair has a life of its own.

Some men solve the hat hair problem by keeping their hair so short that no ridge can form in their hair. In some cases, this can result in hat *head*.

For women, there's no way to avoid a severe case of hat hair if you wear a hat. A ridge will form—and if your hair was nice and high to start with, the top of it will have formed a cone while you were wearing the hat. Combine that with the fluffed sides, and the result is that your hair itself will resemble a hat. Yee-ha.

The solution is simple: Don't remove the hat.

If you're a guy and you want to tip your hat as a sign of respect, you can tip it forward without revealing the hat hair, then put it back on your head.

But ladies, if you choose to wear a hat on a particular occasion, you must be certain that there will be no need to remove it. It must stay glued to your head. (By the way: It's important to make sure your hat is large enough to fit over your hair snugly. If it just sort of perches there and keeps popping off, you'll look quite ridiculous.)

TYPICAL TEXAS HAIRS

Any hairstyle will fly in Texas, as long as it's elevated a little from the way it's worn in the rest of the country.

Texans are pretty hair-tolerant, though if you go for the green spiky kind, maybe you'd better live in Austin.

Here are some of the more popular styles you might choose to adopt:

- **The Mane Event.** This is the big curly one the Dallas Cowboy Cheerleaders like to wear. Huge, long, and curly, this hairstyle is high maintenance. You must be willing to spend approximately 40 percent of your life in pursuit of good hair. When you pack to go some- where, you must be willing to carry a whole piece of luggage for your shampoos, conditioners, blow dryers, curling irons, and volumizing goos. That's the downside. The upside is that everybody will always be talking about your hair. And if you tell a guy you can't go out with him because you have to do your hair, he'll believe you.

■ **The Helmet.** This is unquestionably the most popular hairstyle of wealthy society women in Dallas and Houston. The hair is cut in a sort of bob, but the bob is bigged up, so that it stands a couple of inches away from the face and towers several inches above the forehead. It is smoothed back from the face, then cemented into place with hair spray, so that it will not move in anything less than a Category 4 hurricane. The downside: You must dodge any attempts to run fingers through your hair, because it cannot be done. The fingers will become lodged in your helmet. Extracting them will destroy your hair—and possibly the fingers, too. You'll have to go home and wash your hair. The upside: You can attend one of those excruciatingly long society balls and dance the night away without fear of a single strand getting out of place.

■ **The Helmet with Wings.** This is a modified version of the aforementioned Helmet Hair. In this version, the sides—after they have been teased out a couple inches away from the face—are brushed back in a slight flip, as though you were standing in front of a giant fan and it blew your hair back. Of course, a giant fan would, in reality, completely destroy your helmet. But this sort of blown-back effect is what you're after. What really does the blowing, of course, is your hairdresser's blow dryer. When the wings have been established, he sprays them into place. This style is as immovable as the IRS. Same upside as the Helmet; same downside.

- **Layered Frizz.** This hairstyle seems quite popular in southern parts of the state that are quite humid. The hair is cut into layers. It is allowed to dry naturally, into frizz. This only works if your hair has Brillo-like tendencies. Most women wear it shoulder-length, with the top layers several inches shorter. It's sort of the look a miniature schnauzer gets when it hasn't been groomed in a while. The upside: It's zero maintenance. And it makes all the sense in the world if you live in a humidity-prone area, because if there's humidity, your hair's going to frizz anyway. Trying to tame it is a losing battle. The downside: The Frizz won't play well in the big cities. If you go there, you're going to have to invest in a blow dryer and some de-frizzing goo. (These days there's a goo for everything.)

- **The Wet Poodle.** This is for women with perms—or those few women born with natural curls that actually stay curled in humidity, rather than turning to frizz. You wash your hair. You cover it with gel. You let it dry naturally. The gel keeps it looking wet and keeps those tight little curls formed. You look like a poodle, yes you do, and if you've got one of those cute little Muffy-Puffy names, you're just going to be adorable as hell. The upside: The adorable-as-hell factor, plus the fact that this is far easier to do than the Main Event. The downside: Guys don't like to run their fingers through gel.

- **The Bowl.** Popular among Winter Texans—northerners who spend their winters in South Padre Island and other South Texas communities—this is a low-maintenance do that can easily be maintained by local establishments such as South Padre's Blue Hairing Salon. The hair is cut in the shape of an inverted bowl—sort of like Moe of the Three Stooges. It's blow-dried straight. The upside: It looks great on gray hair, and it is zero maintenance, except for those special occasions when you want to curling-iron it under on the ends. When you wake up in the morning, you look exactly as you did when you went to bed the night before. You can walk down the beach without worrying about having your look destroyed. The downside: It doesn't work unless you have straight hair.

- **The Mop.** This is the hairstyle that results if you give a Bowl cut to somebody with curly hair. The upside: zero maintenance. The downside: You ever see the *Three Stooges* episode where Moe got his finger caught in an electrical socket?

- **Cotton Candy.** This is the hairstyle popularized by former Gov. Ann Richards, although she has since gone on to smaller hair. (This happens sometimes when you're tired of having a high profile; your hair's profile takes a beating, too.) In this style, the hair is swept up in what looks like a giant cone of cotton candy. It works great with white hair, because of the cotton connection. If you have pink or pale blue hair, it would look even more like cotton candy. The upside of the Cotton Candy hairstyle: It's really, really, awesomely tall. The downside: Can't wear a hat with it.

- **Incredibly, amazingly long hair.** There are women in Texas who become accustomed at an early age—say, five—to having really, really long hair and to having people remark on how incredibly, amazingly long their hair is. So they never, ever change it. They wear incredibly, amazingly, long hair—usually completely straight—all their lives. The upside: You develop really good arm muscles blow-drying it. And people are always talking about what amazingly, incredibly long hair you have. The downside: You're always rolling over it with your chair. Other people sit on it. Takes forever to wash and dry. And people who do not have amazingly, incredibly long hair will always be after you to cut it.

- **Incredibly, amazingly short hair.** This is the style that results when a woman is tired of having incredibly, amazingly long hair. You don't see it a whole lot in Texas, despite the fact that it's a valid answer to the humidity problem. But short hair is inherently *small*, and thus, un-Texan. The upside: Your girlfriends will tell you it looks great because you've just reduced your competitiveness in the market for guys. The downside: You'll look like someone Not From Around Here.

- **Fries with That.** This is another hairstyle of habit. Here's the deal: When Fluffy was 15 years old and homecoming queen, she wore her bottle-blonde hair in a cute little flip with bangs. And she has worn it that way ever since. For 50 years, she has had her hair dyed blonde from whatever color it might be. For 50 years she has had it rolled and dried—usually under those big salon hair dryers—twice a week into a perfect flip. With bangs. She wouldn't change it for the world, nor would she permit her hairdresser to. The upside: It's as comfortable as an old stuffed animal. The downside: It kind of looks like an old stuffed animal, and after all that color-processing for 50 years, it's completely fried. Thus the name.

YOUR HAIRDRESSER

Your relationship with your hairdresser is one of the most important you will form in your new home, Texas.

Because hair is such a big thing in Texas, you will spend a lot of time with your hairdresser. You will, together, make that crucial decision on whether your hair should be a Helmet or a Cotton Candy.

You will tell him about your love life. In detail. You will tell him every fault that your boyfriend has and the various ways that you have gotten back at him. You will seek his advice on where to go on vacation and what kind of car to get. He will be invited to your wedding. At Christmas, you will give him a gift—and it had better be a good one if you want that next haircut to work out.

You cannot keep a secret from your hairdresser. It is one of the big rules of Texas hair. You will spend a lot of time in that chair, and you must reveal your entire life while sitting in it.

Breaking up with your hairdresser can be tougher than breaking up with your husband. It's not just that you'll have to find a new hairdresser, though that certainly can be traumatic enough.

Remember: You've been talking to your hairdresser. About everything. And he's going to be mad at you if you leave him, so now everybody in town will know everything about you. Heck, you're not just going to have to find a new hairdresser; you're going to have to *leave town*.

Say, maybe that haircut isn't as bad as you thought.

Chapter 10

DRESSIN' TEXAN

Don't tell me you've read this far and you're still wearing Dockers and button-down white shirts. That cannot possibly be the case, but if it is, do *not* tell me. Just quietly remove your clothing right now. You're starting over.

As a Texan you will, of course, do many of the same things you did when you were an Iowan or Mainiac or whatever you were. You will still go swimming, and you will still wear a swimsuit when you do. You will still play golf, and you will wear a golf shirt when you do.

But for everyday just being, you need to know how to look like you're living in this state, not just passing through. There are several Texas looks. Let's look at those looks:

THE BASIC TEXAN

This is a generic Texas look that is always acceptable in Texas for both males and females. You'll see it pretty much everywhere in the state. The exceptions are Dallas and Houston. But even if you live in Dallas or Houston, you need to learn the Basic Texan look. You'll need it when you play dress-up for western-theme charity balls.

The basic Texas look includes:

- **A colorful, starched, long-sleeved cowboy shirt.** Many years ago, these were only available in white, denim, and black. Now they're every color in the rainbow, all at once. They have beautiful western sunsets painted on them. There is nothing you won't see. Choose any pattern or color. This shirt should be starched so that it can stand up by itself. It's best if the sleeves are a little too long, so that they stand out from your arms. But nothing puffy, you understand.

- **A pair of jeans.** These should be basic blue jeans, and they should be blue. If you're headed for church, dinner, the rodeo, or to meet your date's parents, you should iron a crease into the legs. The most popular style of jeans is the boot cut, which is wide enough in the legs to accommodate your boots. Important: If your jeans are not cut wide enough in the legs to accommodate boots, do not wear boots. Under no circumstances should you stuff your jeans legs into your boots. If you do, you will look like Smokey the Bear, not a Texan. Another warning: Do not hang around with your thumbs hooked into your jeans pockets. The only time you ever really see this in Texas is in regional productions of *Oklahoma!* Ditto with thumbs hooked into suspenders.

- **A belt with a pretty darn big buckle.** The best, of course, are rodeo buckles. They're truly gigantic oval things with the championship you've won engraved on

them. If you're not a rodeo guy, you can buy fake
rodeo buckles at flea markets. Western stores carry a
full line of other large gold and silver buckles, which
you must attach yourself to your belt. Ask your neighbor how. There is one drawback to these big buckles:
When you sit down, they cut into your stomach.
Remember, real cowboys don't have big stomachs.

- **Boots.** You need nice, sturdy boots—probably in cowhide, lizard, or ostrich. Patent leather is not an option. Realize that the first few times you wear these, they're going to be stiff, and you're going to have trouble getting them on and off. Eventually, they will become the most comfortable footwear you own. Your basic boots, to be worn for both casual and dressy occasions, should have a low to medium heel and a fairly round toe, for comfort. Pointy-toed boots are for squashing roaches in corners. Forget about steel toes unless you have some serious ass to kick.

- **A cowboy hat.** It's a must everywhere but Dallas, Austin, and San Antonio. I'll tell you more about cowboy hats later in the chapter.

- **Western accessories.** If you're a man, that generally means a bolo tie (one of those string things with metal ends, clasped together with a silver ornament—something like little guns stuck in tiny holsters —or perhaps a scorpion encased in plastic). If you're a woman it means silver jewelry (earrings shaped like stars or little guns) or rattlesnake jewelry. The bandanna is an accessory that has fallen out of favor. Its original uses were to keep dust out of the eyes and mouth of cowboys and

to disguise bandits. Neither is much of a factor in the average man's dress today. And ever since gang members started wearing bandannas around their heads, cowboys sort of gave them up. The Gangster Look is not covered in this book. Should you, after residing in Texas for a spell, decide to become a gangster, your gang will tell you its own rules. At that point, you may throw this book away—or at somebody you don't like.

OK, this completes your Basic Texan Outfit. You may wear this to work in most parts of the state—the exceptions being Dallas and Houston. You should always wear this outfit when you go to a rodeo or western bar. (Do not wear it to a non-western bar, however, in any major city except Fort Worth. The Basic Texan is always acceptable anywhere in Fort Worth.)

THE PRAIRIE LOOK

This is an option to the Basic Texan available to women. (I say that because it involves wearing skirts. If you're a man and you like wearing skirts, this section is for you, too.)

To achieve this look you will need:

■ **A prairie skirt.** This is a long skirt, but not a floor-length one. It needs to be a few inches off the ground so that people can see your boots, and so things that are on the ground won't crawl up onto you. (This includes small children.) These skirts are often denim, though they can also be gingham or of another

137

drapery-like fabric. Many have a large (and possibly dopey) ruffle around the bottom. If this ruffle should perhaps coordinate with the fabric of your shirt, so much the better.

■ **A shirt with stuff dangling off it.** There are some choices on the shirt. It can be long-sleeved cowboy, short-sleeved cowboy, or just a soft T-shirt or sweat-shirt. The key is in the stuff dangling from it. Conchos—those silver Indian-looking round things— are the most frequently used dangly. Beads will also work, and you can never have too much fringe. An

appliqué of a horse might work. But no tie-dye. This is Texas, not the Haight.

- **A vest.** This should be a patchwork design in as many colors as possible. It should be a short vest, stopping at your waistline, or perhaps above. With fringe or without. It should be coordinated with your dangly shirt. The busier the dangly shirt, the plainer the vest can be, and vice versa. You may wear a dangly shirt without a vest only if it is very thoroughly covered with danglies.

- **A belt.** A concho belt or other silver belt is best. A leather belt with an amazingly large buckle will also work. Or you can wear your shirt loose outside your skirt. Let your stomach be your guide.

- **Cowboy boots or sandals.** Boots are best, but if it's terribly hot outside, be comfortable. Needless to say, wear boots if you're going to be anywhere snakes are.

- **Accessories.** Texas-shaped sunglasses are a nice touch. Dangly earrings, definitely. If they match something that's dangling on your dangly shirt, or if they match your belt, that would be perfect. Silver's the most popular, or earrings made out of rattlesnake rattles.

- **Optional—cowboy hat or wildly decorated sun hat.** Use your discretion here. By the time you've assembled the rest of this outfit, you're probably covered with a dizzying collection of stuff. You don't want to overdo. You may well not need a hat at all. If you do, it should coordinate with the rest of your outfit. If, for example, you have on a pink dangly shirt and a denim skirt, you might try a floppy denim hat with a pink hatband—perhaps with something dangling from it.

This look is appropriate in most rural parts of Texas for everything from church to barbecues. For the Fourth of July barbecues, make sure your outfit is in the colors of red, white, and blue.

THE RHINESTONE COWBOY—MALE

This is a look specially designed for society events that demand city-dwellers dress up as though they were basic Texans. But they're not, so they do things a little differently.

For this look, you will need blue jeans and boots, but wear them with either a rhinestone-studded shirt or a tuxedo shirt and coat. A black cowboy hat completes the look. You're a dandy, and you know it. Now go home and get back into your smoking jacket.

One other thing: If you rarely wear boots, be prepared for great pain if you stand around all night in a new pair. You may have to refuse to dance and deal with any repercussions.

THE RHINESTONE COWBOY—FEMALE

In general, women are advised when they dress up to put on all their clothes and jewelry, then go stand in front of a mirror. Then remove one piece of jewelry. Thus will you be provided with the elegance you're after.

If you live in Dallas, however, the directive changes: Put on all your clothes and jewelry, then stand in front of a mirror. Add one piece of jewelry. That's the look you're after.

You are going to accessorize this jewelry with either a leather or suede dress replete with fringe, or very tight leather pants with a cowboy shirt encrusted with jewels. A cowboy hat is optional, but if you do wear one, be prepared to keep it on all night. (See Chapter 9 for a discussion of Hat Hair.)

A word here about blue jeans and dress codes. The dress code on your party invitation means different things in different parts of Texas. It's this way:

In Houston, Dallas	*In Fort Worth, Tyler*
Casual:	
Black pants with jacket or Dress without cleavage	Jeans and a shirt you don't mind spilling beer on
Dressy casual:	
Black dress (unbeaded), slight cleavage	Long skirt, blouse with conchos on it

Black tie:
      Long, beaded dress,   Long dress, no
      copious cleavage   conchos, slight
                                    cleavage

Black tie optional:
      Cleavage optional   Cleavage optional

Actually, the designation "black tie optional" makes most Texans' teeth grind. It means you have to find out what everybody else is wearing so that your husband won't wind up being the only one in a monkey suit, and you won't wind up looking like Cinderella while everyone else is dressed for church.

Bottom line on the dress thing: Don't wear jeans in Dallas for anything but gardening.

THE TRULY CASUAL TEXAN

In Austin, you can wear pretty much anything you want. If you like jeans, Austin is heaven. There are few restaurants in Austin that you have to dress up to go to, and at one of those I once saw a guy come in wearing shorts and a tank top and get served. I wouldn't recommend doing that at the Four Seasons, of course. But the general attitude in Austin is that if you're wearing shorts and a tank top, you have a very good reason for wearing that, and the decision is one that should be respected.

You are not likely to get frowned at in Austin for what you're wearing. You might get frowned at, however, if you're smoking or going against the flow of traffic in a grocery store.

TEXAS HATS

The good news is that in Texas, you don't have to wear cheese on your head. Don't have to wear a big red pig, either.

What you wear is one of two things: a gimme cap or a cowboy hat.

A gimme cap is a basic baseball cap, though it usually has the logo of your favorite trucking company, tobacco company, or lounge on it. Do not wear it backward on your head if you are over the age of 16. This type of head-wear is good for running errands, sitting around with your friends, or playing baseball.

But the serious Texan headgear is the cowboy hat.

There are many to choose from in just about every price range.

Couple rules about cowboy hats:

- Don't set one down upside down. It could get dirty. It's always best if you can park a hat on a peg rather than have to put it where somebody might mess with it. Many restaurants in Fort Worth and points west have hat pegs.
- Don't put your hat down on a bed. It might get sat on. Besides, it's bad luck.

The hat is creased so that it can be picked up with three fingers and plopped on the head. Watch any John Wayne movie, then try this yourself. Pick the hat up casually with three fingers and plop it on your head so that it rests entirely level on your head—not tilted back. You shouldn't need to stop and arrange it once it's up there. It ruins the effect. Then tug briefly on the brim as a farewell gesture and walk out the door like Jett Rink. Applause.

Chapter 11

VARMINTS AND OTHER LIVING THINGS

You're driving down the road, happily ruminating on what a good a Texan you're becoming when suddenly—whump!—you've hit something.

You alight from your truck to see what it could be. You stare at the remains. Do you recognize this carcass?

You should.

Here are a few of the creatures you're likely to run into in Texas—along with a few you probably won't. If you're lucky.

ARMADILLO

Texas' Number One speed bump. These little guys look like army tanks with long noses. The nine-banded armadillo is the one found in Texas. It's called that because it has nine bands of plates. Check it out if you can find an unsmashed one.

Why did the chicken cross the road? To show the armadillo it could be done. The armadillo just seems to have a tough time getting the hang of it.

Armadillos seem to have a strong attraction to roads. One theory is that they want to get to the other side to look for bugs. (You know how it is: The bugs are always crunchier on the other side.) The 'dillo will be ambling along when suddenly, he sees headlights. Not only does he freeze in his tracks; he does a little jump—just about the time your truck arrives.

Whump! Realignment time.

If you're lucky enough to see a live armadillo on the side of the road, it's probably munching insects. What you're more likely to see is a partial armadillo. The farther south you go, the higher the 'dillo count.

Yes, armadillos can be eaten. They've been barbecued and put in chili. But in order to do this safely, you have to find a live one.

Eating road kill is ill advised.

DEER

You may wonder what happened when you hit an armadillo with your car or truck, but if you hit a deer, you know it.

There are signs all over the Texas countryside that show a deer leaping across the road. Pay attention to these signs. Deer do indeed leap across the road, whenever they feel like it—and they don't look both ways first.

On occasion, a deer's poor timing will result in a collision with a vehicle. The result is invariably great damage to both the car and the deer.

I know of one Texas woman who reacted to this circumstance by getting out of her car, field-dressing the still-warm deer, taking it home, cutting it up, and putting it in her refrigerator.

Don't panic; you don't have to do that. The standard Texas response is to shriek, "Oh no," gnash your teeth a bit, pry the deer off your car, and hope the thing's still driveable. (Your car, not the deer. Chances are high that the deer's mobility has been permanently impaired.) After a few moments of respectful regret for the deer and its family, you may move the deer to the side of the road, go home, and call your insurance company. Good luck.

EMU

Here's something else to look out for in the road.

An emu is a big bird—a relative of the ostrich—that has a long neck and silly little wings that couldn't possibly make the thing fly.

Some years ago, somebody in Texas decided it was a good idea to raise emus. It was explained that emu meat, like ostrich meat, is low in fat and cholesterol. It was believed that one day, the people of this nation would awaken and decide, in unison, that they wanted to eat emus.

So people began buying emus for tens of thousands of dollars apiece. They paired them up, bred them, and produced big green eggs containing little emus. They hatched these and raised these and produced huge flocks of emus. They sold emus to other people who wished to make vast sums of money. Before you know it, it was hard to drive down any Texas highway without seeing a couple dozen emu ranches.

The emu breeders kept waiting for America to get hungry for emu meat. They dreamed of the day that the Emu House would outpace the Steak House as American's prime dining experience. So far, this hasn't happened.

Some emu ranchers still believe that they will someday turn a profit, and they've kept their emus. (There is a niche market for emu oil, which has been said to cure everything from arthritis to itchy skin.)

Other emu ranchers decided that raising emus was for the birds and they—oops—forgot and left the back ranch gate open one night.

The result: Herds of emus roaming the countryside. You may find this funny until the day your truck gets stomped by an angry emu. They have very, very strong feet.

HORNY TOAD

He's not really a toad, and he's not really horny in the way you're probably thinking. These little reptiles are actually lizards. They have bumpy (i.e., horny) skin. The correct term is Texas Horned Lizard. But most people call 'em horny toads or horned frogs. (The horned frog is the official mascot of Texas Christian University, and if you live in Fort Worth, you will see much clothing emblazoned with his image.)

When a horny toad is threatened, he flattens himself out in order to blend in with his surroundings and become invisible. It's a neat trick and very effective—unless the thing that's threatening the horny toad is a car and the place where he's flattening out is the road. In that case, the car completes the flattening process.

BAT

Texas is a batty state.

You won't see bats circling downtown Dallas, but they do inhabit caves, bridges, and, yes, the occasional belfry.

Bats, like other creatures of the night, like to hang out in Austin. I am told there are 1.5 million bats living under the Congress Avenue bridge that crosses Town Lake, but I have not counted them myself.

Go to the bridge at dusk to see them zooming in and out.

If you live in Austin, you're going to have to handle being around bats. Austin is so proud of its bats that it has a hockey team called the Ice Bats. (I know; it sounds like a really bad baseball team. But it's a hockey team.)

I was once in an Austin restaurant where a bat was flying around over the diners. Every now and then someone would look up and remark, "Oh, a bat." But there was no panic. I told you: Austin is laid back.

In general, bats like caves better than restaurants. One cave—Bracken Cave near San Antonio—is said to be home to between 20 million and 40 million bats. Again, this is according to the bat-counters at the Parks and Wildlife Department. You may wish to count them yourself on a dull day.

PRAIRIE DOG

Prairie dogs live in little towns. Isn't that cute?

One primary function the prairie dog serves in Texas is to substitute for the groundhog on Groundhog Day.

There are no groundhogs in Texas, so Texas media events staged on that day must feature a different animal. The Dallas Zoo tried using a snake one year, and the press conference was poorly attended. It was also very difficult to determine whether or not the snake had seen its shadow.

The favorite animal for groundhog substitute seems to be the prairie dog, since it looks more like a groundhog than anything else in Texas. And it does live in the ground—but doesn't hog it.

BADGER

Badgers? We don't need no stinkin' badgers. But we got 'em anyway.

Badgers live primarily in the western and southern regions of the state. You don't want to mess with them. They're not likely to bite you, but they growl and emit an unpleasant aroma if they're stressed.

COW

These are everywhere and, of course, they're not varmints but the most beloved beasts in the state. Virtually every hillside in the state is dotted with these steaks-to-be (except for some hillsides that are dotted with sheep or goats).

As a Texan, you must love cows. It's OK if you're a vegetarian; just don't be too loud about it. If you don't eat the animals, at least look fondly at them.

There are many kinds of cows in Texas, from longhorns to Brahmans. (The latter is pronounced "Bramer." Don't ask why; just do it if you don't want to advertise the fact that you're Not From Around Here.)

It's considered bad form to ask a cattle rancher how many cows he owns. It's like asking how much money he has in the bank.

JACKELOPE

This carefully bred mixture of jackrabbit and antelope lives solely . . . on postcards. Of *course* there's no such thing.

SHAMU

He's the killer whale at Sea World in San Antonio. He never dies. If you're from anywhere that has a Sea World, Shamu lives there, too. Explaining this to your kids is tougher than explaining Santa Claus and his helpers. Good luck.

BASS

It's not officially the state fish of Texas, but it may as well be. Bass-fishing is a revered Texas sport. Get yourself a bass boat. (It's a minimal boat—just a li'l ol' boat with a motor.) Catch you a mess of bass. You'll be amazed at how happy a bass will make you. (These are not to be confused with the Basses of Fort Worth, who are humans—and darn rich ones, too. Do not try to catch these.)

SNAKES

There are about 100 different kinds of snakes in Texas. Boo, hiss.

Among them are rattlesnakes, copperheads, and water moccasins. Watch out for these.

Water moccasins, as you might imagine, inhabit the water. When you go to a Texas lake and see a little reptilian head sticking up out of the water, consider that it could be a water moccasin. It could also be a turtle. Swim very carefully and unsplashily to shore. If it was just a turtle, it'll forgive you for the snub.

Some parts of Texas have so many rattlesnakes that they make 'em into everything from purses to chili. The rattles make attractive earrings.

The town of Sweetwater holds an annual Rattlesnake Roundup, where you, too, can catch rattlesnakes. At the end of the hunt, they fry up a mess of 'em. People who are into Snakes Rights will argue that this type of hostility toward snakes is unwarranted. These people do not live in rattlesnake country.

In certain areas of Texas, roadside rest stops have signs that read, "Watch for snakes." Unfortunately, they don't say what to do if you see one. I would suggest trying to get away unbitten. (Don't make any sudden moves; the snake is likely to think you're going to do something hostile like turn it into a purse, and if it thinks that, it will bite you.)

Rattlesnakes, you probably know, are supposed to shake their rattles before attacking. But they have been known to forget.

Should you see a snake in the road, back up. Ask the snake if it's injured. Regardless of its reply, back over it a few times with your truck.

FIRE ANT

Pronounced *far ain't.*

Fire ants are team players. You never get *one* fire ant bite. What happens is that, in a group, fire ants sneak onto your foot. Then, when the time is right and all ants are aboard, a leader gives the signal: BITE! NOW!

Immediately, your foot will feel like it just got stuck with a thousand burning needles. Ow, ow, ow. You will look down and see a mass of ants on your foot. Get them off, get them off, get them off. Run inside to put something soothing on your foot.

Then go buy some fire ant bait and pour it all over your yard. It should keep the fire ants out until the next rain. Fire ants enjoy swimming, apparently, because after a good rain you will often find a fresh raft of ants in your yard.

Say, I'll bet emu oil feels good on a fire ant bite.

BIG, FLYING COCKROACHES

Remember the part of this book about bigness? How everything is big? So are cockroaches—some of them, anyway.

The good news about these mega-roaches is that they're loners. Unlike German cockroaches and other breeds you may have experienced, these big 'uns just mosey around individually, rather than as a team. Just because you see one doesn't mean you have to call the exterminator. If you see one a day for four days in a row, though, I'd pick up the phone.

These guys are just *nasty* looking. They're a couple inches long, with hairy legs. They like water and dead leaves. So if you have a pool and don't like to rake, get ready for a visit.

You'll be walking across the room when suddenly, out of nowhere, this huge beast of a roach will appear, just sitting there looking at you, waving its ugly antennae.

You will have the urge to go over and step on it.

Don't!

You'll never get that far. When your foot gets within a foot, the roach will suddenly take flight. At you. No Alamo hero was ever more scared than you are going to be at this moment. And there's only one thing to do.

Go get the Raid and drown that sucker. I mean really spray. It's not enough to just get a little on the guy's back. He may wander off and die later, but you won't know that, because unless he's really wetted down, he can still fly. At you. Spray, spray, spray.

And you thought I was hard on snakes.

MOSQUITOES

Texas mosquitoes really aren't much bigger than any-body else's, but they make up for it in meanness. When they bite, they really dig in. And, like fire ants, they often consider biting a team sport.

They will happily chase you from your car to your house, gnawing all the way. Walk quickly and carry a big can of Off.

CRANE FLIES

When you experience your first spring in Texas, you're going to see a flying creature that looks for all the world like a mosquito on steroids. It's huge, has spindly mosquito-like legs, and likes to enter the house.

But, oh happy day, it's not a mosquito. It's a crane fly. It'll annoy the heck out of you, but it won't bite.

BEACH VARMINTS

Oh, yes, there are varmints in and around the ocean too. I'm not talking about sharks, although there are some of those. They tend to keep to themselves around Texas beaches—if they know what's good for them.

Here are the varmints you'll most likely encounter on Texas beaches:

- **Jellyfish.** Moon jellies are the most populous. They just sit there on the beach looking like Vaseline speed bumps. They don't chase you or anything. Kids like to pop them. Don't let your kids do that; they can get sprayed with stuff that stings.

- **Portuguese Man o' War.** These are jellyfish with beautiful blue and purple sails. They sit on top of the waves and drift into shore. Below their bodies hang long tentacles that sting. It is these that are responsible for most beach stingings. Watch for them as you're jogging down the beach. The baby ones will get you too. And, yes, the dead ones can sting. (And hey: How do you know who's dead and who's not? We're talking jellyfish here.) There are two tried-and-true remedies, by the way, to take the pain out of a jellyfish sting: meat tenderizer and ... um ... pee. My advice: Keep a shaker of meat tenderizer in your condo or hotel room. (Don't count on getting stung, though. Odds are you won't, unless you really like molesting jellyfish that have run aground.)

- **Sea gulls.** Sea gulls are perfectly nice, white birds that go ee-ee-ee and make you feel like you're at the beach. On the other hand, they're the pigeons of the sea. This is important: If you want to be a Texan and you want to be liked, when you're on the beach—and especially when you're around your condo or hotel—do not feed the gulls. Immediately dozens of them will show up and relieve themselves upon the heads of your fellow Texans, who will, at that point, be ill disposed to buy you drinks.

- **Spring breakers.** These are college students who infest the beaches during all of March. They don't sting and they don't (usually, anyway) relieve themselves on your head. But they have a loud mating call ("PAAAAAAAAAAR-TY!") and they crowd up the bars and restaurants. They should be approached with caution.

Chapter 12

SO YOU WANT TO BE A COWBOY

First thing you have to decide is: which kind?

Do you want to be a football-playing Dallas Cowboy or a hat-wearing Texas Cowboy? And of that second kind, there are several varieties:

Do you want to be a yee-ha, hat-throwing, bull-riding, bowlegged rodeo cowboy?

Or do you want to be a ranch cowboy—the kind that actually messes with cows?

Or do you simply want to have enough cowboy in you to pass for a Texan when you're out of state?

We'll go over all four, but unless you have special qualifications, I'm going to suggest you go for the fourth option—at least, for now. We can all dream.

THE DALLAS COWBOYS

The words Dallas and Cowboy, when used in combination, always refer to football players, because there are no other kinds of cowboys in Dallas. There are cowboys in the Dallas suburb of Mesquite, where there's a rodeo. But Dallas, Texas, has as many cowboys as it does oil wells: Zip. So if you want to be a Dallas Cowboy, you're talkin' football. Here's the lowdown on that occupation:

You will need: Large body (unless you aim to be a kicker), uniform, pads, helmet, football, million-dollar contract, and a basic hatred for the media.

How to be one: Let's get right down to brass tacks:

Do you know how to play football? Are you really, really good at it?

Didn't think so. Let's move on to Option No. 2:

RODEO COWBOY

You will need: A rope, a hat, some very tight jeans, and a large can of spray starch. It also helps if you do not consider your brains your best feature, because you're likely to get them stomped out at some point.

How to be one: How old are you? Most Texas cowboys start rodeoing (yep, it's a verb too) when they're just kids. They start with an event called the Calf Scramble. It's an event where they release a herd of calves, then they release a herd of kids. The kids run after the calves and try to catch them and drag them to a specified area.

At this point, you find out if rodeo is even a vague possibility for you. One of my daughters tried the Calf Scramble when she was about six. She saw all those calves running and promptly fled in the opposite direction. She did not become a cowgirl. She became a Mary Kay beauty consultant.

Little kids can proceed from this event to actually riding on some of the larger calves—who won't like it and will try to eject them, just as bulls will later in life. Or they can try riding horses that haven't been broken and get thrown off by those same broncs. If they enjoy this sort of abuse, they're rodeo material.

And I mean cowboys enjoy it a lot. If a bull-rider gets to the rodeo and winds up having to ride a bull that doesn't make every effort to kill him—what cowboys call a "rank" bull—the cowboy is disappointed. (He also gets low scores. Bull-riding is easier if the bull is not trying to kill you.)

The best of these rodeo cowboys compete for cash prizes and belt buckles. They pay entry fees for the privilege. If a cowboy's wearing a huge belt buckle with writing on it, he's probably won some rodeos. Either that, or he's shopped enough flea markets to make himself look the part.

If you're 40 years old and want to start being this kind of cowboy, you'll need to give the matter a great deal of thought. Consider the following qualities of rodeo cowboys, and see if you measure up.

A rodeo cowboy:

- Must look good in very tight jeans. Because that's what they wear—the kind with the legs that fit over their boots. Because these jeans-encased legs spend a great deal of time gripping the sides of an animal, after a while both the legs and the jeans develop a natural bow. The legs begin to resemble parentheses. Would you like your legs to be parentheses? And, specifically, will your rear fit nicely into a pair of jeans—no ifs, ands, or butts?

- Must like starch. You will be wearing beautiful western shirts, and they will be starched stiff enough to stand up all by themselves. Allow one can of starch per two shirts. Spray, spray, spray. You think your wife sprays her hair a lot? She'll need to spray your shirts a lot more. Or, if you haven't found a wife yet, you or your girlfriend will need to.

- Must not be too fond of brains. I mention this earlier, but I reiterate it here because not only must *you* not consider your brains your best feature; your wife must feel the same way. She should admire you for your taste in shirts, the way you stay on that bull for eight seconds, and the way you look in tight jeans. But she can't be too awfully fond of your head.

- Must have strong legs to grip horses and bulls with.

- Must have a crooked, aw-shucks kind of smile.

- Must be polite at all times. After that bronc throws you and you get up and dust off and go back behind the chutes and this cute thing comes up to you and asks how you are, and you feel like you've just been in a train wreck, you will smile that crooked smile and say, "Just fine, ma'am. Can I get you some lemonade?"

You don't, by the way, have to be a long, tall Texan in order to be a rodeo cowboy. Short guys tend to make great cowboys—maybe because they don't have so far to fall.

A word about women and the rodeo: At this point, the big women's event at rodeos is barrel racing. That's where you ride your horse at full gallop around barrels in a figure eight, then race back to where you started. Why is it that women don't routinely compete in bronc riding and bull riding? Could be a lot of gender discrimination. But I prefer to think it's just because women value their brains.

165

So, OK: Do you qualify to be a rodeo cowboy, you think? If so, give the Professional Rodeo Cowboys Association a call and stock up on spray starch.

If, on the other hand, you value your brains, let's move on to Option No. 3:

RANCHING COWBOYS

Ranch cowboys also need hats, but they can wear their jeans looser. They do have to work, but their brains are less at risk.

You will need: A truck and some cows (they don't have to be your own cows.) A horse is also nice.

How to be one: This may disappoint you, but these days, most ranchers rodeo in their trucks, not on horseback. It depends on the terrain, of course, but especially in South Texas where the land is mostly flat, it's silly to get your horse and yourself all sweaty when you can ride in an air-conditioned truck.

Of course, when you get together with other cowboys, it's nice to be able to ride around on a horse. It's something that cowboys generally enjoy. Many ranching cowboys are also rodeo cowboys. The choice is yours.

But the chief qualification for being a ranching cowboy is that you have to like being around cows. This is tricky: You need to like the cows, but you don't want to become *friends* with the cows.

Let's not lose sight of why those cows are there. They are not pets. Eventually, they will be hamburgers and prime rib. Thus, naming the cows is probably a bad idea. It will cause you to weep when ol' Ralph goes off to the grinder.

Here are some common questions and answers about cows and their tending:

What is the difference between beef cattle and dairy cows?

Beef cattle make steaks and dairy cows make milk. Beef cattle are generally stockier livestock; they have shorter legs and are heftier-looking—the better to make steaks with. Dairy cows have great big udders full of milk all the time. If a beef cow has an udder full of milk, it's because she just gave birth to a calf. In Texas, there are more beef cattle than dairy cattle.

This seems like a good place to bring up all that cow-print stuff that's popular up north. It's black-on-white cow print, and that signifies a Holstein cow. Holstein cows are dairy cows. Nothing riles a beef cattleman more than somebody sending him something with a Holstein motif. It's like sending a painting of a bunch of apples to an orange grower. It's not harmful; it's just irrelevant.

What is the difference between a bull and a steer?

In a word, testicles. Steers don't have them. And most males of the bovine family become steers. The bull has been specially selected, through careful breeding, to be a really excellent dad. So when he is born, he is allowed to hang onto the family jewels. It is expected that he will have many, many love affairs in the pasture. If he doesn't, he's dog food.

167

How do you attract a cow's attention?

Rattle a feed sack. Or do a really good impression of a bull.

What happens to the cows when they're out in the pasture and a rainstorm hits?

They get really wet. Hey, that's life if you're a cow.

And there's really no reason to get upset about it. The cows don't get upset. They are aware, in their own cow-awareness way, that having to stand around in crummy weather is part of their cowness. When a really bad Texas storm hits, they just kind of huddle together and deal with it. They don't even know they're at any sort of risk.

And that's good. Because when there's a tornado warning, you sure don't want them stampeding into your bathroom and throwing your mattresses over their heads.

Do Texas cows have mad cow disease?

Nah. Anytime a Texas cow gets mad, it's probably something the bull said.

The mad cow disease, of course, was at the heart of the Texas cattlemen's lawsuit against talk show host Oprah Winfrey. She did a show on mad cow disease, and it scared her, and she said she wouldn't eat any more hamburgers.

So the cattlemen sued, saying she'd libeled beef. They got their case thrown out in Amarillo. It wasn't that the Amarillo judge didn't like hamburgers; it was just that if you can libel a product that easily, there are a lot of little Texas schoolchildren who should be in jail for the things they say about their vegetables.

Anyway, none of this really did much to scare us carnivores away from beef. You can't swing a dead 'dillo in Texas without hitting a steakhouse.

How do ranchers know where their cows are?

They don't always. They know they're somewhere in the pastureland they put them on. Probably. (There are occasional cattle rustlings, but that's still considered one of the most heinous crimes in the state. I wouldn't advise it.) The ranchers know the cows won't cross a cattle guard—steel bars across a ditch. (They're afraid they'll break their heels; we can identify with that, can't we, ladies?) And they know the cows can't usually get through barbed wire (pronounced *bobwar*) fences. Every now and then, a cow somehow manages to transport itself out into the middle of the road. If a rancher sees such a thing, he's honor bound to check the brand or ear tag and figure out whose cow it is, then either take the cow back or at least call the guy and let him know. The rest of us just honk at the thing and scare it half to death.

Ranch cowboys have to work very hard making sure cows are where they're supposed to be, eating what they're supposed to be eating, and living the way they should be living.

But the reward is that they get to spend a lot of time outside developing that weathered cowboy look. The romanticized cowboy of the movies is a guy who sits out under the stars at night and just loves sleeping on the ground. (The ground is hard. Just thought I'd throw that in, in case you plan to try this.)

Because ranch cowboys have historically spent a lot of time hanging out under the stars, many have developed an artistic streak. They are poets and singers.

Let's mention, at this point, that women can be ranch cowboys, too. And they really can help out when everybody's sitting around the campfire trying to think of something that rhymes with "heifer."

You may think you have no poetic bent until you get out there under the big sky—nothing but you, the sky, the cows, and a snake or two. All this may inspire you to write poetry.

Or not.

If it does, though, the cowboy poets I know seem to agree on one thing: The stuff better rhyme. Nothing's worse than a free-verse cowboy poet who writes his name all in little letters like e.e. cummings.

Singing is easier.

It's always fun to sing around a campfire, while riding the range in your truck, or while drinking with fellow cowboys. Learning to harmonize is also a good idea. And if you are tone deaf, for God's sake learn to play the harmonica. Somebody has to do that.

Some good cowboy songs to sing:

- "Whoopie Ti Yi Yo, Get Along, Little Dogies." (Please note: It's dogies, not doggies. Doggies are the things that bark. Also, this is just a song to be sung. Don't go around yelling "Whoopie Ti Yi Yo!" or the other cowboys will look at you funny.)
- "El Paso." Learn the words off a Marty Robbins tape. If you also happen to play the guitar, you can show off your virtuosity with this one.
- "Cool Water." This one will make you thirsty as heck if you're not around any water, so you may want to save it for a time when you're out under the stars and right next to a nice clear stream. Or a cooler full of beer.

■ "Tumblin' Tumbleweed." Yes, it does seem rather silly to sing about tumbleweeds "pledging their love to the ground," but believe me, cowboys take this song very seriously—and they take tumbleweeds very seriously, too. You'll learn why if you ever get one caught in your truck's undercarriage. This is a pretty song and highly worth singing.

■ "Ghost Riders in the Sky." More yippee-i-ay, yippee-i-yo stuff.

■ "Cowboy's Lament." Also called "Streets of Laredo." Contains the famous line: "I see by your outfit that you are a cowboy." And, yes, if you get an outfit you can be a cowboy, too. If outfitting—and not cows—is what you're really after, please proceed to Option No. 4:

SEMI-COWBOY

Call it drugstore cowboy or just the Texas look. This is probably what you're after, pardner. It's a harmless form of cowboy that doesn't get you all hot and sweaty—unless you want to be.

You will need: A hat. Boots.

Let's look at this realistically. You are now a Texan, so any time you go anywhere else in the world, they're going to assume you're a cowboy anyway. May as well play along.

In Chapter 2, we went over the names you could give yourself now that you're a Texan. There's one I didn't mention, and that's because, in a way, we all have that name:

Tex.

When you live in Texas and you go someplace outside of Texas, no matter what your name is, people are going to call you Tex. They just can't help themselves. You can try all you want to explain that you live in Dallas and that there are no cowboys in Dallas. You can also explain that you don't know a soul in the state of Texas named Tex.

They will call you Tex.

They will also yell "ya-hoo," because they don't know that the proper word is "yee-ha."

And when the time comes to pay the bar tab and you ask if you can settle up, the bartender will say, "Saddle up! Ha Ha Ha!"

So you may as well be a cowboy.

You've read Chapter 10 on Dressin' Texan, so you know all about the hats and boots. And you have at least one of each. OK, *two* boots, one hat.

OK, put on a pair of jeans. Pull on your boots. You can either wear a starched long-sleeved cowboy shirt or a short-sleeved cowboy shirt. Add a bolo if you like.

Now put the hat on. That's right, flat on your head, not cocked back like some Yankee afraid of messin' up his hair.

Check your face in the mirror. Is it weathered? If not, you're going to have to spend some serious time outside in the sun. You can go horseback riding, play golf, lay out by the pool, or even go to the tanning bed (but don't tell anybody). But to look like a real cowboy, you can't have a perfect alabaster complexion. It just doesn't work. Don't overdo; skin cancer is not necessary. But a little cragginess is mandatory.

Once you have achieved the leather-skin look, stand in front of the mirror again. Stand with legs apart—no, not like you're ready to draw at the OK Corral, just casually *standing around*, waiting to see if anybody wants to make trouble. Good.

Look in the mirror again. Assume the attitude. Grin crookedly. Leer lazily. Stare menacingly. Let your eyes grow cold, as though you just heard some fightin' words. There you go. You've just run through your facial repertoire.

You don't have to practice any particular type of speech. Just use your basic Texan lingo and remember: Cowboys don't talk much. When they do, they talk slowly and—unless riled—politely.

It is important to decide at this point whether or not you're going to bother to learn to ride a horse. This matters, because if you ever visit a ranch and you have on your hats and boots, people will expect you to be able to ride a horse.

If, on the other hand, you plan to spend the rest of your life living in Dallas—and you plan to travel only to such places as New York, Chicago, Los Angeles, Paris, and Peking—you can probably fake it without ever going near anything that says "neigh."

If you do plan to do any riding, though, it's a good idea to take actual riding *lessons*.

You don't need many—just enough to know how to get on a horse (without a ladder, yes), how to hold the reins, how to guide your horse with your knees and body language, and what to do when your horse takes off racing down a mountain. Hint: Grabbing the saddle horn and shouting, "Stop! Stop! Stop!" will not do the trick. I learned this the hard way.

The proper stop command for a horse is "whoa." Not that saying this will necessary cause the horse to stop. But it works better than any other words you might extemporaneously decide to scream into its ear.

You have to develop a relationship with the horse that tells the horse you know what you're doing up there. You're in charge. You *like* being on a horse's back. You are comfortable there. All this must be telegraphed to the beast by the way you sit, move, and talk.

If the horse thinks he's the first horse you've ever ridden, he's going to get off on getting you off.

Also, don't take one lesson and assume you are John Wayne. Long trail rides are for people whose rear ends and inner thighs have built up calluses through years of horseback riding.

One more note on rear end conservation: Don't trot.

OK, so you've had a lesson or two and don't feel as though horseback riding is life threatening. You still might want to avoid horses with names like Diablo and Jet. Experience indicates that those names weren't just pulled out of a hat.

RHINESTONE COWBOYS AND COWGIRLS

Perhaps you live in Dallas or Houston and the only time you need to dress up like a cowboy is once a year when you go to the Cattle Baron's Ball or some such.

Just a few notes on western parties:

You don't need to know how to ride a horse, and actually, alabaster skin *will* work with this look. Everybody knows you're not a cowboy anyway, so you don't need to look like you've been out riding the range.

Guys, just slap on some jeans, boots, and a tuxedo shirt.

Ladies, you're going to have to make a choice. Are you going for high glitz or comfort at this western party? Because the most popular thing for women to wear to these things is a suede or leather dress. And if you do this, there are two possibilities: (1) It will rain and you'll wind up smelling like a wet cow or (2) It will be hot, you'll sweat and you'll wind up smelling like a wet cow.

A nice cotton shirt and long skirt might feel—and smell —a whole lot better.

THE COWBOY WAY

Whether you ride the range on a horse or just haul ass in your truck, you've probably learned by now that there's a little bit of cowboy in all us Texans.

We're polite and friendly. We stand up for what we think is right. We have boots to keep our feet firmly on the ground and hats to keeping our heads cool. We walk tall, talk tall, and live tall. Heck, even our hair's tall.

Welcome to the big ol' world of being a Texan. It's not hard. It's all just (clap, clap, clap, clap) deep in your heart.

Chapter 13

SCHOOL DAZE

If you have kids—or if you *are* a kid—then you're going to care about getting educated in Texas. And we have good news about that: It can be done.

Your Texan child, unless you send him or her to a private school, is going to be enrolled in something called an I.S.D.—which stands for Independent School District. The school districts of Texas are independent of the cities in which they are located. This means they levy their own taxes. This they do with great relish. In case your realtor failed to tell you—and they do sometimes overlook this little fact—Texas homes are assessed at full market value. That's supposed to be exactly the amount you would get for the house if you sold it. What it winds up being, of course, is about 125 percent of what you would get for the house if you sold it. Disputing your tax bill on that basis, however, will get you nowhere. It is also fruitless to offer to sell your house to your local assessor for what he seems to think it's worth. Using any of these arguments pegs you immediately as someone Not From Around Here, because people from here know this is just how things are. You get your tax bill, and you pay it.

One of the reasons you are not supposed to mind paying it is that little Buster will get himself a pretty fair education for the money you pay.

ELEMENTARY SCHOOL

Here is something you will need to break gently to your kids: The Texas school year starts smack in the middle of summer. Your child will be scarcely more than a week into August when he will find himself sitting in a schoolroom. A generation ago, prior to air-conditioning, school started during the first week of September. But now that the schools have air-conditioning, they want to use the heck out of it. So during the hottest days of the year, school's in.

The upside is that during the school year your child will have miscellaneous days off, including a week-long spring break. And in general, school lets out the last week of May.

None of that is going to make the kid happy about going to school in August. But off he will go, to learn all about the Alamo.

With him you must send:

■ A backpack like all the other kids' backpacks. Ask a sixth grader which kind is popular this year.

■ A three-ring binder that is exactly the kind your school wants. If you school wants one with a three-inch-wide spine and your kid's is two inches, he will be publicly humiliated. Check the list the school gave you when you registered him, and do not deviate from it in the least.

■ The exact type of tablets and pencils specified by the school. They demand certain brand names, certain colors of ink, whatever. Everybody's everything must be alike.

■ A box of Kleenex. They never tell you why you have to send this, but you do. I think the supposition is that your kid is going to get a cold, and when he does, out comes the box of Kleenex. If it's a particularly healthy year for the children in your school, they can always build a homecoming float with the leftovers.

MIDDLE SCHOOL AND JUNIOR HIGH

Some Texas districts follow elementary school with middle school, and some follow it with junior high.

Middle school and junior high are very scary things. The girls are tall, and the guys are short. The girls are developing sexy voices. The guys' voices are different every single day. (My heart goes out to junior high school choir directors.)

The girls are aggressive, and the guys are aggressive, and they just don't know what to do with all the newfound raging hormones. So generally, they just hit each other a lot. Don't be alarmed if your school principal calls asking for a conference because young Coy or Charlene got in a fight. Junior high kids are not really sure how to reveal their emotions. They hit people they don't like; they hit people they like. This is true the world over, but especially in Texas, where nobody takes any guff off anybody else.

Bottom line: This is not a good time in life to buy your child an automatic assault rifle.

Junior high and middle school are also when school officials start getting serious about dress codes. Some schools are stricter than others, but in general, those cute little shorts the kids wore to elementary school are banned in junior high. Shorts and skirts have to be a certain length. And schools just hate the heck out of hats. For some reason, headgear just really sets them off. Probably because of this, junior high boys can't really live without caps. Grab it off your kid as he leaves the breakfast table.

Regardless of whether your child goes to middle school or junior high, grades 10 through 12 are high school, where things get pretty serious.

Sports are serious. This will be discussed at length in the next chapter.

And proms and homecoming are serious.

You have not seen pomp and circumstance until you have seen high school special events in Texas.

The homecoming football game is followed by a dance, so most girls wear long, semiformal dresses to the game—along with a (trumpet fanfare, please) corsage.

The corsage is such a big deal that it almost merits its own chapter.

Think back, please, to your high school homecoming and the mum that your boyfriend pinned on you.

Compared to that, the mum your daughter is going to get is the flower that ate Pflugerville. It is the Godzilla of gardenias. This is no corsage. This is a float. It wears the girl, not vice versa.

What it'll be is three big mums—fake ones, because they keep these for years—with a huge bunch of streamers that reach from the shoulder to the hemline of your daughter's dress. Or maybe to the floor, if she's short. Or maybe they pile up around her feet, if she's really short, and they trip her all night. Appended to this floral apparatus will be several dozen plastic footballs, streamers that say "Bubba and Bubbette '99," bells, pom-poms, musical notes, plastic footballs, and stars. Somewhere in there, a stuffed bear will be nestled. All this, your daughter will *wear*. When she walks, she will sound like a cow, and yes, the weight of the mum will tear a big hole in her dress and leave her slope-shouldered.

But wait—what if he's a boy? What if you have a son, and he has to buy this thing? Think $75 and up. Seriously. Or his girlfriend will never speak to him again.

The girl buys the guy a lapel flower, too—and it's about the size of the mum girls used to wear in the '60s. At last check these ran about $20.

That was homecoming. But prom is bigger. Happily, you don't have mums at prom. The girls are given tasteful wrist corsages, because they've usually spent their family's monthly food budget on a dress, and they don't want to get a big hole in it.

Often, several couples will get together and hire a limousine to take them to the prom. There, they will dance for about half an hour, then demand to go out to an expensive restaurant to dinner. Afterward, there is often a party at a hotel (assuming there is a hotel in your town). It's an all-night deal. It drives hotel night managers and police crazy. But this is Texas, and proms are done big, like everything else.

You've seen the movie *Giant?* The scene at the end of Jett Rink's party is a good approximation of prom night in Texas.

Oh, yeah—somewhere during high school, stuffed between all the parties, there are classes. These are attended, more often than not, and enough education is absorbed to propel your child into either life or college.

At this point, it is time for graduation.

If you're from a state that considers graduation a solemn occasion, you must rethink the situation. In Texas, your son or daughter will think you don't like him or her if you forget to bring your air horn to graduation. The thing is one big pep rally. There are speeches, but they are short. There are long lines of graduates tromping across the stage, and when your child's name is announced, your entire clan—including granny from Montana, who has been airlifted in for the occasion—must stand and make as much noise as possible. You will only have a few seconds, and your son or daughter will not be allowed to react. Texas schools like the words "zero tolerance" and have adopted "zero tolerance" policies for just about everything, and that includes excessive exuberance at graduation. Little Coonrad cannot yell "All riiiiight!" and backflip off the stage. Diplomas have been yanked for stuff like this. That means it's up to *you* to make a fool of yourself on behalf of your offspring.

COLLEGE

It is not unlikely that your child will want to go to college in Texas. The state actually has some great schools, and state-supported colleges are downright cheap compared with those of many other states.

There are some well-known private universities as well. The biggest of these are:

- Southern Methodist University in Dallas, known for its Meadows School for the Arts and its very rich, very blonde female students. Many Dallas men have been known to select their brides from this fairly deep pool. Sororities and fraternities are extremely big on this campus. The athletic teams are Mustangs. A very sad thing happened to the SMU football program in the late '80s. Because of recruiting violations, the school received the "death penalty" from the NCAA, which meant no football at all for a year. A T-shirt featuring a horse with its feet up in the air was minted, but few had the audacity to wear it publicly. SMU's been trying to rebuild ever since.

- Baylor University in Waco, probably best known as the biggest Baptist school in the state. It was well into the '90s before the board of trustees allowed dancing on campus—and then it was stipulated that wild gyrations would not be permitted. And, indeed, no lascivious behavior seems to have resulted from the new Dancing Bear Rule. In general, kids who attend Baylor tend not to be gyration prone. Still, it's one small two-step for mankind. There's an old joke popular in the Bible Belt (which this is, in case you hadn't noticed): Baptists can't make love while standing up; somebody might think they're dancing.

- Rice University in Houston, known for its Ivy League-like academic programs. The mascot is, aptly, the owl. Still, these are no geeks. The Marching Owl Band—the MOB, for short—is one of the state's smallest collegiate marching bands, but certainly the one with the driest

wit. It's not really a marching band; members *run* into
formation and are known for such maneuvers as
marching backward and electing a refrigerator homecoming queen.

■ Texas Christian University in Fort Worth, known for
having the strangest mascot in Texas, the horned frog.
A purple horned frog, at that.

Respected Texas state-supported colleges and universi-
ties include Texas Tech in Lubbock, University of North
Texas in Denton (known for its Grammy-winning One
O'Clock Lab Band), and Stephen F. Austin University in
Nacogdoches, along with dozens of branches of the Uni-
versity of Texas and Texas A&M.

The big University of Texas is, of course, in Austin. And
Texas A&M is in College Station. And between these two
cities fly the sparks of a rivalry unequaled anywhere in the
country.

THE RIVALS

There is no school anywhere with as fierce a spirit as
Texas A&M University. The students are the butts of count-
less Aggie jokes, but they take themselves seriously. And
they really can't stand the University of Texas, which they
sneeringly refer to as "T.U." (Frankly, this confounds
alumni of the University of Texas. TU? What, Texas Utili-
ties? Most Longhorns don't feel too wounded.)

Each year Aggies prove the ferocity of their spirit by
building a bonfire, which has been measured at 55 feet

high. It consumes more than 5,000 logs and represents the school's burning desire to beat the University of Texas in football. (In recent years, when deforestation became an issue, A&M students began planting seedlings to replace the wood consumed in the bonfire.)

Other Aggie traditions include the team mascot dog Reveille, who wags his tail on the sidelines during games, and the legendary Aggie "twelfth man" on the football team. The twelfth man is said to be the embodiment of Aggie spirit.

My husband, a newspaper columnist, once wrote after a particularly devastating Aggie loss, "the twelfth man missed the team bus." He got a scathing letter from the Fightin' Aggie Band, which threatened to show him what the twelfth man spirit was all about, should he ever set foot on campus.

Now that's scary. Imagine being literally drummed out of town.

The Fightin' Aggie Band, of course, is known for its musical and marching prowess, not its sense of humor. Once, during an A&M game against Rice, the aforementioned MOB played a spirited rendition of "Oh Where, Oh Where Has My Little Dog Gone." The dog whom A&M had designated as Reveille that year had just died. The Aggie band was not amused, and concession trucks had to be called in to disperse its members, who were ready to go to war with the MOB.

Then there's the fighting slogan "Gig 'em, Aggies," which is accompanied by a thumb stuck in the air, out of a closed fist. There is a Web site on the Internet that advocates erecting on campus a huge statue of the "Gig 'em thumb," which looks more or less like a hitchhiking thumb. I state this not derisively but as a simple fact. I would not want the Aggies to think I am making fun of them. Thumbs up, guys.

Just as A&M has its Reveille, the University of Texas has its mascot, Bevo the longhorn steer.

In 1916 a bunch of Texas alums got together, pooled their money, and bought a steer. I'm not sure what his original name was. But a couple years after he was purchased, the Aggies briefly stole the beast and painted the score of the game, 13-0, on him.

This was meant to embarrass the Longhorns, and it did. So they took some more paint and carefully crafted the score into a word—Bevo.

Bevo's been the sacred cow ever since.

UT fans are no less rabid than Aggie fans. When they win a game, the huge tower in the middle of campus is lit up in the school color, burnt orange. (The other school color is white, but there'd be nothing special about lighting the tower that way, would there?)

UT alumni consider Austin a shrine and frequently wish to live out their lives there. (If you live in Austin, don't go around bragging about having a UT degree. Everybody has one, including your waiter.) More than one UT alum has named his kid Austin. The tyke should count himself lucky he didn't wind up being Bevo.

UT kids have stolen Reveille from time to time, but their favorite weapon is the Aggie joke. Here's another one, just in case you've forgotten what they're like:

What's the difference between Aggies and Rice Krispies? Rice Krispies know what to do in a bowl.

Of course, those denizens of Austin have been a little soggy in the bowl lately, too.

Chapter 14

SPORTS IN TEXAS

Do not ever, under any circumstances, use the words "It's only a game" in Texas. If a game is being played in this state, its outcome is serious bidness.

In fact, when my ex-sportswriter husband and his friends learned I was to include sports in a humorous book about Texas, they were aghast.

"Sports," they said, "is serious."

So please affix a grim look to your face and read on.

The most serious sport of them all is football.

Football is the quintessential male bonding experience. You're banging into each other, you're sweaty, and you're guys. Doesn't get much better than that, does it?

So it is that you'll find television sports broadcasts leading with the fact that a particular football player has developed a head cold, while stories about major world soccer championships and baseball games are pushed later into the newscast.

There is an elementary school in East Dallas where, on any given day, you can find a touch football game going on. This has been happening for forty years. There are some pretty old guys in these games. They just can't let go.

High school football *rules*.

The spectators are merciless. Losing is something that isn't handled very well in the state of Texas.

As for the players, you know the old saw about having to be a football hero to get a beautiful girl. It's true. There's no easier way to get popular than to play high school football.

But being a football hero is not easy in Texas. Texas is, as you know by now, hot. Practices under the broiling sun are arduous. There used to be summer practices, but those have been abandoned in the interest of health.

"Air Force basic training was nothing compared with summer football," grouses my husband, who once played the game but didn't really get along with it—because it was played outside in the heat, and because my husband has never really liked getting pounded. Football hurts. The other hard part of playing football was getting his shoulder pads stuck in the window of the school bus while he was kissing his drill-team sweetie good-bye on the way out of town. But we'll leave the exploration of that topic for another book, another time.

Texas creativity rears its head in the naming of these high school football teams. Sure, there are the usual Wildcats, Bears, and Lions. (For some reason, no one seems to have chosen the Cheetah.) There are Spartans and Trojans and such.

But we also have the Hutto Hippos, the Taylor Ducks, the Port Lavaca Sand Crabs, the Winters Blizzards, the Itasca Wompus Cats, and the Trent Gorillas. For a while, the girls' sports teams in Trent were known as the Gorillaettes. (Is that better or worse than the girls' teams at Central Junior High School in Euless, who are known as the Lady Stallions?)

Friday nights in the fall in Texas are the sole property of high school football. Large, Astro-turfed stadiums are not at all unusual. If a high school is too small to field a regulation team, it plays six-man football. There are many dozens of these teams in the state, and they are sanctioned for schools of less than one hundred students. (West Texas is chock full of these.)

How much does this state love high school football? Just a few examples:

- One football coach in Big Sandy was elected mayor. Fact is, most coaches of successful teams could be elected mayor—at least—but they wouldn't want the job. They have their priorities in order. This guy did, too. He quit the mayor job after a while. It was interfering with football.

- One town got in trouble for supplying football players with vitamins and paying all their medical bills.

- In the '70s, a Houston construction magnate shelled out $18,000 to send Huntsville High School to Alaska, where the team had been invited to play what was to be known as the "Santa Claus Bowl" against Anchorage High School. Huntsville won, which made Texas happy. It didn't please Alaska, though, and no Texas team has been invited back.

- There was a legendary team from Breckenridge High School in West Texas in the '50s. This team was a powerhouse—a consistent state champion football team. These were the days of the oil boom, and Breckenridge had oil, so it had money. Its coach was among the best paid in the state. When Breckenridge had an away game—and away generally means far away in that part of the state—the town emptied. But there were always some people who couldn't get away. So the guy who owned the local drive-in theater arranged to broadcast the Breckenridge High School football games at the drive-in. People showed up just after dawn to stake out their spots.

- There was a kid who lived in nearby Moran who was a really good player. His dad was a teacher. Breckenridge wanted this kid on its team. So the school district offered the dad a job. "Nah, that's OK," said the dad.

"We're happy where we are." The family went on vacation and returned to find that their house had been moved inside the Breckenridge city limit.

Such is the devotion to high school football within Texas.

The seriousness of college football is most evident in the rivalry between Texas and A&M, which we covered in the last chapter.

As for pro football: Nobody goes as nuts as Texas, especially Dallas. (You may recall that Houston once had a professional football team but lost it. The result was the creation of the Tennessee Oilers, which makes about as much sense as the Utah Jazz.)

How 'bout them Cowboys?

If you live in Dallas and haven't yet heard that rallying cry, it must be spring, and you must be a new arrival. It's how you'll be greeting your coworkers every day when you arrive at work throughout the football season.

If your coworker emits the cry first, the correct reply is "Yeah!" or "Um!" or some sort of positive grunt. You are under no obligation to dissect the most recent Cowboys game. It's just a greeting, is all.

You'll probably be offered a square in the office betting pool. Take it. You do want to be one of the guys, don't you? (Even if you're one of the girls, you still want to be one of the guys.)

The Cowboys are called—by Dallasites, anyway—America's Team. America sometimes calls them that, except for the times when they stop winning and have a bunch of players thrown in jail on drug offenses—then they become known as South America's Team.

A big, big thing to remember in Dallas: Tom Landry is a saint, and former quarterback Roger Staubach isn't far behind.

Tom Landry, of course, is the first Dallas Cowboys coach, beloved by everyone. Even when his team stopped winning in the '80s, everybody loved Tom and hated to hear unfavorable things about him.

Jerry Jones bought the team, fired Tom Landry, and hired Jimmy Johnson. Jimmy Johnson won the Super Bowl twice in a row. That's nice, and the fans liked Jimmy Johnson.

But they still *loved* Tom Landry. And still do, some coaches later.

As for Roger Staubach, he is a reminder of the days when the Cowboys were considered gentlemen and football players. They were winners on and off the field. Roger became a successful businessman in Dallas, and quarterback Troy Aikman—who now owns, among other things, a car dealership—is following in his footsteps, although he will never achieve sainthood.

One other note about Dallas football: It's played in Texas Stadium, which is enclosed except for a hole in the roof through which, it is said, God can watch his favorite team play. Great, but if it's hot, everybody gets hot and if it's wet, almost everybody gets wet. The guy who designed the stadium made a point of making it impossible to ever get a retractable roof over the thing, so it looks like it'll always be that way. If you're headed for a Cowboys game on a day of less-than-perfect weather, dress accordingly.

BASEBALL

Baseball, though not as big a deal as football, is right up there, thanks to the Texas Rangers (who play in Arlington) and the Houston Astros (so named because of the huge space complex NASA built in Houston.)

Baseball is a good sport for Texas, because it's so warm most of the time. The downside is, of course, that warm turns into hot so much of the time. Despite the heat, fans will attend games in droves *if their team is winning.*

If not, your stadium tends to empty out.

Texas baseball players, while they rearrange themselves just like all other baseball players, don't like to let you see them sweat. They handle the state's heat well and are rarely seen mopping their brows.

And they're patient. The Rangers have been known to rain-delay a game for more than three hours, then pick up where they left off. It'll be left to the statisticians to figure out which day the game was played on.

One of the greatest Texas Rangers moments anyone can remember involved legendary pitcher Nolan Ryan. The Rangers were playing the White Sox that day. Ryan hit Robin Ventura with a pitch, and Ventura, to the astonishment of everyone in the stands, charged the mound. He didn't even get a punch in. The middle-aged pitcher put Ventura in a headlock and went to work. The headline in a Houston paper the next day read: "Ryan Throws 6-Hitter."

The Rangers and Astros hold their fans' attention well, but as of this writing, neither had won a pennant, much less a World Series. And neither seemed in danger of doing so. Thus, when a Rangers game and a Cowboys game are played on the same day, it's usually the 'boys who take precedence on the big-screen TVs in town—of which there are very, very many.

One more little baseball note: There's a minor league team in San Antonio whose mascot is a puffy taco. Looks real cute running the bases.

BASKETBALL

Yes, the round ball gets respect in Texas too, though a bit more in Houston than in Dallas.

Although talented high school basketball players aren't nurtured the way outstanding football players are (that's how Oak Cliff's Dennis Rodman and San Antonio's Shaquille O'Neal got away), the University of Houston has made a name for itself as a training ground for hoopsters.

Akeem Olajuwon, Elvin Hayes, and Clyde "The Glide" Drexler all graduated from the University of Houston and all, at one time or another, played for the Houston Rockets.

Olajuwon was a happy accident at U of H. The Nigerian showed up at practice in a cab, wanting to try out. He made the team, and aren't we all glad?

Texas team performances have been spotty. In 1966 Texas Western (now the University of Texas at El Paso) won the NCAA championship, upsetting the University of Kentucky. But there hasn't been a Lone Star national college champ since.

And the pros? Led by Olajuwon, the Houston Rockets won NBA championships in 1994 and 1995 (not coincidentally, the years that Michael Jordan was out of action).

If you live in San Antonio, go see the Spurs. They've done well for themselves in the David Robinson years. The Rockets have a loyal following in Houston. The Dallas Mavericks have struggled, struggled, struggled. But hope springs eternal, and perhaps the new Dallas sports arena will provide some motivation. If not, maybe a course in remedial basket making.

HOCKEY

If you're from one of the very cold states, you are probably a big ice hockey fan.

Texas is trying to get excited about ice hockey. The Dallas Stars have done a lot to advance that cause. It's been a real struggle. Bubba and his pals just aren't real sure they should get excited about a bunch of guys on ice skates chasing a little puck.

But they sure do like the fights, and that may be what finally wins Texans over to hockey. You cannot, of course, play hockey without having brawls. Some of the Stars have been known to take boxing lessons to improve their abilities in this area. Brawls are good ol' Texan things. So ice hockey is developing a following. No doubt you'll go to a fight one night, and a hockey game will break out.

SOCCER

Where this sport is concerned, Texas is like most other states: Little kids are flocking to soccer like lemmings. Everybody—girls, boys—plays this game. And like everywhere else, soccer moms are the most rabid human beings you will ever come across.

"You @#$%, move your @#$%#4!"

That was a mom talking to her own kid.

It's a strange sport in that respect, but the kids seem to play it anyway. Few, however, grow up to have any interest in soccer.

Dallas Morning News columnist Blackie Sherrod is of the opinion that kids play soccer so they won't have to watch it. Sure seems that way, considering adult Texans' disregard for the sport.

World Cup Soccer raises little but yawns in most parts of Texas. Only people who have moved here from Europe or South America give a hidy-ho.

On the TV news, the winner of the World Cup will be announced only after the day's baseball scores and—of course—something about football, even though it's not football season.

When nonessential World Cup games were played in Dallas' Cotton Bowl several years back, a restrictive cyclone fence was put up to prevent possible riots. Riots? In Dallas, over soccer...during the summer? Yeah, right.

You're a soccer fan? During the World Cup, take a vacation to a place that cares.

TRACK AND FIELD

Quoth one sage sports observer: "If there's anything I hate more than track, it's field."

These are second-tier sports here, like everywhere else, even though the state has produced more than its share of national champions. High school athletes often run track because they have to, as part of their participation in athletics.

Still, since Dallas is the home of Olympic gold-medal winner Michael Johnson, known as the world's fastest man, you'll see more respect for track meets here than in some other states.

And Texas has had other major players on the track and field scene. Olympic champs have included long jumper and sprinter Carl Lewis, shot putter Randy Matson, high jumper Louise Ritter, and sprinter Bobby Morrow. So running and jumping are alive and well in Texas, if that's what you want to do.

FISHIN'

Fishing is still one of the most laid-back outdoor activities in America, but it's probably a little more intense in Texas than in most states. Here, people seem to care a little more about actually catching fish. Not that they don't enjoy just sitting by a cooler of beer all day long with a line in the water; it's just that if you don't catch a fish, you don't have anything to talk about later. And talking is a big-time Texas sport.

Most Texas freshwater fishing takes place in man-made lakes. There is, in fact, only one natural lake in all of the huge state of Texas—and most of that one, Caddo Lake, is actually in Louisiana.

Freshwater fishing is generally great in this state, especially in East Texas. If you stay after it, you'll catch lots of bass. Anything over 13 pounds is generally referred to as a lunker. And stripers—striped bass—have been known to go over 30 pounds in Lake Texoma, on the border of Texas and Oklahoma.

There's a little fish known as a crappie, and you should know that it's pronounced "croppie." That will keep you from getting into trouble if you wish to report you've been taking large crappie behind the boathouse.

Those big, long fish that look kind of like alligators are called gar. They're trash fish with teeth. Cut 'em loose.

Saltwater fishing is great for sea trout (increasing in recent years), redfish, snapper, drum, and even an occasional sailfish or tarpon, though I wouldn't get my heart set on one.

If you like deep sea fishing, there are plenty of boats that go out of Galveston, Port Aransas, and Port Isabel (across the causeway from South Padre Island). If you tend to get seasick, you might want to opt for a half day of bay fishing, where waters are generally glass-calm. Once you're two hours out on the Gulf of Mexico, you have to deal with whatever the ocean feels like doing that day. The fun of deep sea fishing, of course, is that you never know what you're going to pull up—anything from a shark to a stingray, along with some stuff you'll never identify. It's a sea bound version of poker.

HUNTIN'

Let's get this out of the way: Hunting is a sport accomplished with a gun. If you're going to hunt, you're going to have to use a gun. If you don't like guns, try a different sport. But do not try to persuade Texas hunters not to use guns. They're not going to suddenly start shooting quail with cameras.

Regardless of whether you, yourself, wish to hunt, you are going to hear a good bit about hunting in Texas. It's a popular sport, ranking just below football for a large segment of the Texas population.

Have you eaten venison or other wild game in your favorite big-city restaurant? It's quite possible that your chef bagged the game himself. Chefs seem to like hunting.

The first clue you'll have that you're around hunters is that you'll start hearing things like "four-ten," "deer lease," and "deer blind."

A .410 is a shotgun, not a football call.

As for the deer lease: This was a mystery to me for quite some time. I couldn't imagine why anyone would lease a deer when you can buy one outright at tremendous savings.

They don't. A deer lease, as it turns out, is a piece of land that tends to be frequented by deer. The owner of that land leases it to various hunters so that they may hunt the deer. A deer lease is a great thing to have, because almost all of the hunting in Texas takes place on private property.

The lease is a precious commodity. In a Texas divorce action, who gets the deer lease is a factor "ranking just below child custody and above the country club membership," says Dallas hunter Tom Stephenson, who knows.

If you don't have a deer lease, call the Texas Department of Parks and Wildlife or the Texas Wildlife Association. They'll tell you how to get a basic license and where to go hunt cheaply.

A *deer blind* is a small building that hunters hide in so the deer won't see them. That way, they can get a better shot at the deer.

These days, hunters are supposed to wear bright orange stuff instead of camouflage clothes. I know, I know: It's not as much fun and doesn't feel as cool. But if you don't wear the bright orange stuff, you could get shot.

Wise Texas hunters wait until the end of the day, when they're all back at the hunting lodge, to get seriously drunk. But unwise ones go ahead and get drunk while they have guns in their hands. These are in the minority, but a dangerous minority they are.

Farmers who live near deer leases get pretty darn tired of seeing their cows get shot by tipsy hunters. One guy even painted the word COW on the side of his cow. She got shot anyway.

It's not as if there aren't enough *deer* to shoot. White-tailed deer are on Texas like a blanket—probably more in Texas alone now than in the whole thirteen original colonies when the Declaration of Independence was signed.

The opening of deer season in Texas (the first Saturday in November) is an amazingly big deal. If your car breaks down that weekend, you're out of luck. Nobody's going to fix it. Everybody's off hunting deer. So you may as well join 'em.

What do you do once you've shot you a deer? First, you figure out how good a rack of horns the animal has. There is an antler-scoring system among Texas hunters that only they understand; you'll have to ask one. But a certain type horn is awarded a certain amount of points, and if you score, say, a ten-point buck, your friends will be very proud of you.

Then you take the deer to a deer processing plant. There's one of these in virtually every central and south Texas town. In goes the deer: Out comes the venison and venison sausage and what not.

The deer's head, of course, goes on your wall so it can glare at you. (Sunglasses can cut down on the glare.)

What do you hunt for in Texas, besides deer? Doves, quail, wild pigs (javelinas), quail, ducks—even snipes. Yes, there is such thing as a snipe. It's a little bird that doesn't move very fast and doesn't taste very good, but it does exist and can be hunted, if you can't find anything else.

And lest you think hunting is a low-rent sport: Shotguns are sold in Dallas for as much as $50,000 at a store in Highland Park Village. Hunters proudly wear camouflage cummerbunds with their tuxedos. There's even a stretch limo Jeep tooling around the state. You can get into this as extensively as you want to. Women, you too. There are many female hunters in Texas, particularly during the start of dove season, which is a major social event. Usually, their husbands get them interested in it.

If your husband takes you hunting, consider it a good sign. He's counting you as a keeper.

GOLF

Texas is home to such golfing legends as Ben Hogan, Byron Nelson, and Lee Trevino. But each had to learn that Texas golf is a little different from golf in other states.

I hate to belabor the point, but it's hot here. In the summer, it can be many weeks—sometimes months— between rainfalls. The best sprinkler system in the world has trouble keeping up with a severe drought. So you're not going to see the thick, lush greens and fairways that you see in some more temperate climates. Your ball is likely to roll a little faster across the green (or the brown, if it's been a really long time between rains and your city has issued a watering ban).

But, of course, the good part is that you can play great golf in December and January. Send pictures to your friends in New York and Michigan.

One more thing about rain: It's traditional for it to fall on the annual Byron Nelson golf tournament in May. Some years it may be the last rain you see until September.

HORSES

This is not Kentucky. You won't see acres of green horse farms around here. But no need for a long face: Texas has great respect for the noble beast, and several ponies from here have run in the Kentucky Derby.

Horse racing is developing great popularity, with the newest and biggest track—Lone Star Park in Grand Prairie—drawing crowds from across the state and beyond.

The heat is hard on the horses, but you—unless you are a jockey—can sit in air-conditioned comfort for a very reasonable fee while you cheer, and bet on, your favorite horses. And Grand Prairie is near Dallas, so when you win a pile, you can go out to dinner somewhere really nice and blow it all.

People are always wondering what to wear to the horse races in Texas. The tracks aren't really dressy, but you're going to get some frowns if you show up in the Jockey Club wearing shorts. In the grandstand, of course, they're mandatory. Dress depending on where you're sitting, but do wear comfortable shoes. You'll be wearing a path to the betting window.

One other sport that's grown in recent years is cutting-horse competition. This is sometimes a rodeo event, but there are a good many events, especially in Fort Worth, that limit themselves to cutting. Such stars as Tanya Tucker have developed a fondness for this event, which involves you and your horse working as a team to herd cows. The most difficult part is staying on the horse.

CARS

The racing of cars has long been popular in Texas, but only with the arrival of NASCAR races at Fort Worth's Texas Motor Speedway has it moved from being primarily a television sport to one where large quantities of Texans actually get in their own cars and head for the races.

Sure, there have always been smaller tracks. And they've had their loyal followers who have spent their weekends watching the cars go around and around.

But TMS is big, and its bigness makes people feel comfortable who wouldn't normally go to a car race. Maybe it's the safety-in-numbers thing. Whatever: Every weekend that there's a big race at this speedway, cars back up for many miles. It can take several hours to drive 20 miles, and if beer is consumed during these miles, a problem can develop. Roadside relief has caused some complaints from people who live along Texas 114.

Race drivers A.J. Foyt and Johnny Rutherford are Texans, so there is a good racing tradition in the state.

But the point of going to a car race, of course, is not to see a lot of little cars go around and around and around. It's to see them crash. And some usually do. So a good time is had by all, then all get in their cars and plod home, same way they came.

Actually, if you're looking for high crash quotient, you might be able to have just as good a time sitting in a bar overlooking Central Expressway in Dallas.

YOU BE THE COACH

In a way, we're all coaches of whatever teams we live near. Be it the San Antonio Spurs, the Houston Rockets, or the Dallas Cowboys. Radio sports talk shows have made experts of us all. Call in with your two cents worth.

There are so many of these sports talk shows in Texas that you can't turn on your radio without hitting one. The guys who host these shows—guys like Norm Hitzges and Randy Galloway in Dallas—have become household names. They're stars, even though a lot of people don't know what they look like. More people know what Galloway looks like, because he also has a newspaper column. But one of the most recognizable *sounds* in Dallas is the Norm Hitzges giggle.

So these people get on the radio every day, and they introduce a topic—say, the Cowboys defense—and you call them and tell them what you think.

"The defense sucks."

"Why do you say that, Albert in Arlington?"

"Well, they're not getting the job done; they just need to focus and get in there and hit some people."

Heck, you keep talking like that, you can handle post-game interviews. You have registered your opinion, by gum. It's probably one you picked up from Galloway's morning column, but it is now your property.

And next week, if the Cowboys defense *does* get the job done, you can take credit.

LIFE AFTER SPORTS

Some sports are not for the old. Or the middle-aged. Or the slightly-older-than-kids. And somehow this happens faster in Texas because—I hate repeating it, but it's true—it's just really hot here.

Face it: Not long after a guy turns thirty in any major pro sport (except maybe golf) people are going to expect him to decline and be a little disappointed if he doesn't. The exceptions that prove that rule, of course, are people like Michael Jordan and Nolan Ryan.

But in football, for example, even if you're still sharp mentally, your hands can still catch, and your feet can still run, you're going to start getting tired eventually. And if you don't, your younger colleagues are going to be angry about that, too.

That's the pros. As for you and me, Mr. and Ms. Not-Too-Athletic-To-Start-With, we really have to accept our limitations. You used to be a great runner? Don't overdo in the Texas sun when you're fifty years old. You could once cram volleyballs down the throats of every bum on the beach? Pick your bums carefully now.

My own husband learned his limitations many years ago. He was a champion high school high jumper. So a dozen or so years after high school, one night, after enjoying some cocktails, he set about proving that he could still high-jump.

He was not on a field at the time. He was on a parking lot behind a bar. He decided to get his friends to hold up a parking sign. This he would jump over. They did, and he did. They raised it; he jumped it. He was doing great and feeling fine. He was a champion.

Then, finally, they raised it to a point where he wasn't sure he could clear it. Still, that old competitive Texas spirit refused to die. You can do it, it said. So he ran . . . and jumped . . . and cleared the parking sign! My hero! Then he landed on his elbows, both of which broke. He spent the next several weeks in huge casts.

Do yourself a favor. At some point, let that old competitive Texas spirit die. Go play shuffleboard.

Chapter 15

RAH, RAH, RAH

In a state that takes its sports seriously, you would expect that people would also take cheerleading seriously. And you would be right.

How seriously do Texans take their cheerleading? Seriously enough that the mother of a Texas high school cheerleader once hatched a murder plot against the mother of another high school cheerleader right before that year's tryouts. The thinking was that the daughter of the murdered mom wouldn't do very well at tryouts because she'd be sad.

Sound logic aside, the plot fell through and the would-be murderous mom wound up in jail. This was juicy stuff, and two made-for-TV movies emerged from the incident. Nobody remembers which daughters wound up making the cheerleading squad, though, and that's unfortunate. Because being a cheerleader is to a Texas girl what being a football player is to a Texas boy: really, really important.

Little girls—tiny ones or several years old—will be seen practicing cheers in their front yards. (Why practice in the back yard? Nobody can see you there.) There are organizations of kiddie cheerleaders who cheer for nobody in particular, but they do cheer, so that they can compete against other cheerleaders. Smile. Cheer. *Kill.*

To be a high school cheerleader is to be the girl next door whom everybody loves. Cheerleaders don't just think they're better than everybody else. They *know* they're better than everybody else. High school cheerleaders in Texas are expected to be perfection personified—pretty, smart, perky, and, of course, drug-free. (They'd better be. They get tested, just like air traffic controllers.)

That means when cheerleaders are out of town they are liable to attempt to transform into normal teenagers. This rarely works. When cheerleaders are caught breaking laws—curfew infractions, for example—they're liable to immediately break down, 'fess up, and reveal their real names. They just don't have much practice at being bad, so they're bad at it.

Cheerleaders are expected, above all, to be relentlessly cheerful, so heaven help the girl who gets depressed for a nanosecond. It's just not tolerated. You have to be out there, smiling and yelling and doing Herkies, perky as all get-out.

Ah yes, Herkies. This is the Texas-patented maneuver in which you extend one arm, put the other on your hip, and jump with one leg straight and the other bent. It was invented by a man from Dallas named Lawrence Herkimer, known as "Herkie," who was himself a cheerleader and later founded a company making cheerleading uniforms.

The ultimate cheerleader, Herkimer was well known for years in Dallas for attending society events in a tuxedo embellished with diamond-encrusted studs shaped like megaphones. He was still jumping at parties when he was in his '70s.

Although few cheerleaders look like Herkie, most would kill to be that perky.

Texas cheerleaders, of course, have bigger hair and curlier bangs than cheerleaders from other states. If the squad decides to wear ponytails (and it's an all-for-one thing, you know), their ponytails will be bigger and bouncier than anyone else's.

Other athletes may not know that cheerleaders take private lessons. They must learn to tumble and jump. They must learn to shake their tails. And they must learn to do their makeup, complete with Vaseline on the teeth to avoid the coat-hanger-in-the-mouth look from all that smiling.

213

They must attend cheerleading camp at SMU, where they will learn to be perky and as blonde as possible. It's hard, darnit. And expensive. (What's all this talk about TWO BITS?)

Still, it's what every girl wants to be. When squad lists are posted after tryouts, fights have been known to erupt in the parking lot. Not among the cheerleaders. Among the moms. Behind every cheerful cheerleader there's a mom who's first runner up to Lady Macbeth. This, of course, inevitably leads to things like the mom who tried to have the other mom killed. This story didn't surprise Texans in the least. It's amazing it doesn't happen more often.

DRILL TEAMS

Once considered cheerleader wannabes, drill teams have now come into their own as performing dance troupes. And Texas was in the vanguard of this movement many years ago, because its premier troupe has always been the Kilgore Rangerettes.

The Rangerettes, under the auspices of Kilgore College, are cowgirls. They wear cowboy hats, boots, and little red and white flare-skirted uniforms. Not sexy. Texan. They're famous for their high-kick drills and are invited to be in just about every parade in Texas.

I saw them in a Cotton Bowl parade once. Unfortunately, they were placed right after a group of horses. The Rangerettes bravely kicked, danced, then finished by doing splits in the road. Those uniforms were no doubt rushed to the cleaners while the girls were still on the bus back to Kilgore.

THE DALLAS COWBOYS CHEERLEADERS

All young cheerleaders, of course, aspire to grow up into major league team cheerleaders. And the greatest of these are the Dallas Cowboys Cheerleaders.

The job of Dallas Cowboys Cheerleaders really doesn't have anything to do with cheering for the team. Have you ever seen this bunch do an organized "Gimme a D" bit? Nah. They dance. They're dancers. They jump up and down and look pleased when the Cowboys score, if they happen to be watching the game, but cheering is not their principal job.

They are a (fanfare, please) symbol.

Cowboys owner Jerry Jones sure learned this the hard way.

The Cowboys Cheerleaders, most people believe, helped make the Cowboys into America's Team by being so gorgeous and sweet. In 1976 a TV camera at a Cowboys game caught the Cowboys Cheerleaders doing one of their routines. A cheerleader winked at the camera, and a nation fell in love.

A 1978 movie called *Debbie Does Dallas* made the cheerleaders mad because it implied that cheerleaders were earthy li'l ol' things. In fact, the cheerleaders were held up as angelic emblems of American virtue. Sure, they were beautiful, had big hair, showed their navels, their legs, their cleavage, and an eensy bit of their rear ends, but they were virtuous young ladies, darn it, and nobody better say otherwise.

So along came Jerry Jones to buy the Cowboys. In 1989, after he'd made a bunch of changes in the Cowboys organization, he decided he'd like to make some changes for the Cowboys Cheerleaders. For example, he wanted to make their uniforms a little skimpier. He also thought it might be nice to banish the rule against cheerleaders dating Cowboys personnel.

The cheerleaders were outraged. We are virtuous young ladies, they said.

Yeah, OK, you are, said Jones. He tried to make amends by referring to them at a press conference as "the pick of the litter." Wrong approach.

Now the cheerleaders were *really* mad. They were, they said, symbols of goodness, and their uniform was "like the flag."

Jones knew enough to back off and leave the cheer-leader uniform thing alone. Things seem to have gone fine ever since.

HOORAH, EVERYBODY

Cheerleading is a sport in which amateurs can participate.

There's a guy named Crazy Ray who, years ago, decided he was going to help the Dallas Cowboys Cheerleaders lead cheers. So he put on a fringy rhinestone cowboy outfit (wouldn't you love to have a cowboy outfit-making plant in Texas?) and showed up at a game. He got in front of the stands and proceeded to cheer. Everybody cheered for him. So he cheered even more. Soon he was considered a part of the team. When he was injured during a game, he was hauled off in the helmeted vehicle reserved for ushering wounded players off the field. He became a legend in his own mind, then crossed over into a real legend.

It's that simple.

You've seen the guys with weird face paint dancing around on the bleachers at a baseball game? That could be you. You'd get on TV that way. You can be a cheerleader. All you need is a gimmick.

Of course, in a way, all of us Texans are cheerleaders. When we're out of town and somebody says something about Texas, we are prone to speak up proudly—possibly even belligerently—in favor of our state.

Sometimes, of course, that works to our detriment. My husband and I were in a cab in San Francisco one day when the Dallas Cowboys were playing the 'Niners. The cabbie asked where we were from. Dallas, we said. He screeched the car over to the side of the road.

"Get out!" he demanded.

Our enthusiasm for our homeland was, of course, undi-
minished. There is no prouder group of people than
Texans. And that includes those of us who weren't born
here but got here as fast as we could.

A common piece of advice in Texas: Never ask a
stranger where he's from. If he's from Texas, he'll tell you.
If not . . . well, you don't want to embarrass him.

Rah.

THE TEST

Oh, you didn't know there was going to be a test? There is. Here it is:

1. The state song of Texas is:
   (a) "The Eyes of Texas"
   (b) "Texas, Our Texas"
   (c) "The Yellow Rose of Texas"
   (d) "All My Exes Live in Texas

2. Which of the following things should you *not* do if snow is forecast?
   (a) Wring your hands.
   (b) Stock up on canned corn and duct tape.
   (c) Gather materials for the making of a snowman.

3. Which is least likely in Texas?
   (a) a white Christmas
   (b) a tornado
   (c) winning the Texas Lottery
   (d) remembering the words to the state song

4. Which of the following is a good name for a Texan?
   (a) Maurice
   (b) Algernon
   (c) Tex
   (d) Godfrey

5. A Texas woman named Puffy Star Jones is likely to be:
   (a) fat
   (b) rich
   (c) available
   (d) employed as an actress

6. The plural of *you* is:
   (a) y'all
   (b) youse
   (c) Aggies

7. If you tump into a tank, you:
   (a) drink out of the city water tower.
   (b) siphon gas from your neighbor's car.
   (c) fall into a pond.
   (d) cut down on your Pearl beer consumption.

8. You have run over your neighbor's cat. What gait do you use to go next door and report it?
   (a) the amble
   (b) the beer-carryin' trudge
   (c) the cut 'n' run: Get the heck out of there!
   (d) the Texas two-step

9. What is the most important thing for you to haul in your pickup?

10. Which of the following does *not* belong on the truck of a Texan?
   (a) a gun rack
   (b) an "I don't eat animals" bumper sticker
   (c) a dog in the truck bed

11. Trophy wives are always:
   (a) stupid
   (b) expensive

(c) young

12. Your Texas mutt is a good dog because:
    (a) He will come no matter what you call him.
    (b) You can enter him in dog shows.
    (c) He loves you.

13. Which of the following belongs in chili:
    (a) corn
    (b) beans
    (c) meat

14. Mexican food is:
    (a) easy to make.
    (b) best made by real Mexicans.
    (c) served in all cafeterias.

15. Which of the following is *not* a good Texas threat?
    (a) I'm gon' kick yer ass.
    (b) I'm gon' buss yer head.
    (c) I'm gon' tell yore mama.

16. Bubba has six enemies. Three have been insulting his wife, two have disparaged his dog, and one has been looking at him funny for several days. How many cans of Whup-Ass must Bubba open?

17. A Texas woman's hair must be:
    (a) big
    (b) huge
    (c) high
    (d) flame retardant
    (e) all of the above

18. How do you prevent hat hair?

19. A Texan's jeans must always be:

   (a) tight
   (b) relaxed-fit
   (c) blue

20. In Austin, you should wear:
   (a) stuff from the resale shop
   (b) stuff from the Gap
   (c) whatever you feel like wearing
   (d) a wrist corsage

21. If you see an armadillo, he:
   (a) will hide behind a tree.
   (b) will have his little feet pointed to the heavens in rigor mortis.
   (c) will attack.

22. Which of the following is most likely to ruin a picnic?
   (a) horny toads
   (b) fire ants
   (c) crane flies
   (d) mayonnaise

23. Which of the following is *not* a quality of a rodeo cowboy?
   (a) He is polite.
   (b) His legs are shaped like parentheses.
   (c) He has a large neck.

24. Which of the following is *not* a cowboy song?
   (a) "Louie, Louie"
   (b) "El Paso"
   (c) "Tumblin' Tumbleweed"

25. Bevo is:
   (a) the nickname of the governor of Texas.
   (b) the mascot for the University of Texas.

224

(c) what you yell while dancing the Cotton-Eyed Joe.

26. Reveille is:
    (a) the first-chair horn-player's trumpet in the Fightin' Aggie Band.
    (b) the top song on the Aggie Top 40.
    (c) the Texas A&M mascot.

27. Football is to Texas as:
    (a) Rocky is to Bullwinkle.
    (b) ink is to pen.
    (c) scissors are to paper.
    (d) pie is to fried.

28. You need a deer lease because:
    (a) you don't own one outright.
    (b) you want to hunt for deer.
    (c) your friends will laugh at you if you don't have one.

29. What is a Herkie?

30. Who is a Herkie?

31. Are your black-eyed peas done yet?

THE ANSWERS

1. (b)
2. (c) It's not going to snow *that* much.
3. (c), but give yourself half credit for (d). It's not out of the question.
4. (c)
5. (b)
6. (a)
7. (c)
8. (c), though if you insist on going over there, (b) is the best idea.
9. Ass
10. (b)
11. (b), but the other two don't hurt.
12. either (a) or (c)
13. (c), and if you missed this one, you automatically fail the test.
14. (b)
15. (c)
16. Just one. It's all a Texan ever needs.
17. (d)
18. Don't wear a hat.
19. (c)

20. (c)
21. (b)
22. (b)
23. (c)
24. (a) It's a sailor song, silly.
25. (b)
26. (c)
27. (b) You're one of those hot shots who got 1600 on your SAT, aren't you?
28. either (b) or (c)
29. a cheerleading jump
30. the guy who invented the Herkie
31. Yes. If they're not, you must be reading this book by the Evelyn Wood method. Go back and take your time.